WestBow Press books may be ordered through booksellers or by contacting:

WestBow Press
A Division of Thomas Nelson
1663 Liberty Drive
Bloomington, IN 47403
www.westbowpress.com
1-(866) 928-1240

Because of the dynamic nature of the Internet, any web addresses or links contained in this book may have changed since publication and may no longer be valid. The views expressed in this work are solely those of the author and do not necessarily reflect the views of the publisher, and the publisher hereby disclaims any responsibility for them.

Any people depicted in stock imagery provided by Thinkstock are models, and such images are being used for illustrative purposes only.

Certain stock imagery © Thinkstock.

ISBN: 978-1-4497-1864-0 (sc)
ISBN: 978-1-4497-1865-7 (hc)
ISBN: 978-1-4497-1863-3 (e)

Library of Congress Control Number: 2011930619

Printed in the United States of America

WestBow Press rev. date: 6/10/2011

Royalty Reigns

In the Grand Scheme of Things

Angela Yvette

WestBow
PRESS
A DIVISION OF THOMAS NELSON

Dedication

To my parents, who tirelessly and sacrificially raised us in the admonition of Christ. Thank you.

Epigraph

In all thy ways acknowledge him, and he will direct
your paths.
—King Solomon

Preface

"With God we will gain the victory, and he will trample down our enemies" (Ps. 108:13). The devil thought he had defeated us, but in *Royalty Reigns: In the Grand Scheme of Things*, we are still standing— standing on the rock of God.

Introduction

It was the symmetry of her sway that attracted him to her. And it would be the balance and beauty of their union that would keep them together. Dad always said that it was Mom's hula hooping skills that attracted him to her. Why not? She was a young, svelte, and beautiful fifteen-year-old girl who was voluptuously balancing and rotating a wide tube around her ten-inch waist. One realizes that mere interest becomes a conception while wanting to take physical action dominates the aforethought.

Celeste Zather (my mom) and Janet, the girlfriend of Celeste's brother, Art, loved to hula hoop. It was one of the hip things to do in the '70s. And on a hot summer day in small-town Cambridge, Indiana, listening to Motown hits, gossiping, and perfecting one's hula hooping skills were the hippest things for fifteen-year-old girls to do. But this day was a little different. Fine Mr. Preston Carnegie (my dad) was driving along with his friends and noticed the pretty and petite pubescent gyrating a hoop around her waist. Janet acknowledged my dad; but Dad acknowledged my mom. Although Preston was good-looking, Celeste ignored him.

Here was this six-foot-two-inch, Native American-looking, slim, perfectly smiling, and chiseled eighteen-year-old guy trying to get Mom's attention, but she rejected him. But it was in vain. Dad was always the charismatic, proactive, and handsome go-getter. Either he was trained that way, born that way, or purposed to be that way. Simply put, he was spoiled and if he wanted something, he would get it. Preston wanted Celeste, and he got her.

Dad introduced Mom to the fast life: parties, booze, and sex. He charismatically swept her off her five feet and one inch stature, and would endlessly take her mind, body, and soul. Nonetheless, Dad insisted that it was the love they shared that prompted a marriage proposal. Needless to say, a year after the initial meeting on the hill and subsequent pregnancy, they planned their eternal union. But first, Dad had to be introduced to my maternal grandma, Bennie May Zather.

"You don't have to marry my daughter just because she is pregnant." Those were Grandma's first words when told of the impending marriage of her baby girl to her beau. Grandma Bennie was a strong, Southern, spirit-filled woman who brought her five children, Rod, Jocelyn, Art, Celeste, and Monte, and her two nephews, Walt and Jack, north up from the red dirt hills of Georgia. After the untimely death of Grandma's husband, she saw departure to a better life in the North as the only recourse.

My maternal grandpa was accidentally shot and killed by a relative on July 4, 1946. Mom, who never knew her dad, would use this tragedy as a reason for her adamant and poignant belief in keeping the family together, no matter what.

Despite Grandma's admonition to wait for marriage, Mom and Dad prevailed. As they proceeded down the aisle (as witnessed by the Zather and Carnegie families, neither of whom in any way, shape, or form appreciated the other), not only was it the beginning of their oneness, but the first addition to their union, Angel Yvonne Carnegie. Over the years of their marriage, they would add my siblings Caren, Tonya, Preston II, Felicia, Grover, and Katie.

It all started with me. I was their seed in the beginning. Psalm 128:3 reads, "Your wife will be like a fruitful vine within your house: your sons [and daughters] like olive shoots around your table." Children and family are a blessing from God. My siblings and I have grown to become beautiful blossoms. With growth come inquiry, insight, investigation, and some devastation. These are the notions that have shaped me into the person that I am today and would in turn shape the rest of the Carnegie clan.

I inexorably, infinitely, and unconditionally love my parents. Make no mistake. But I have a story to tell. The following account involves love, supernatural intervention, sex, intrigue, deception , sin and forgiveness. But the greatest of these is love. First Corinthians 13:13 reads, "And now these three remain: faith, hope, and love, But the greatest of these is Love." Hear it, feel it, learn from it.

CHAPTER 1

Caren, the second-born child to Preston and Celeste, and Jerry Zather, my cousin, child of maternal Auntie Joycelyn, were always being scolded, punished, spanked, apprehended, you name it; they were always in trouble. She was five, he was nine, and I was eight. At that time, we lived with Grandma Bennie. This was one of our many intra-family stops we would make as our principal provider, Dad, relentlessly worked to give his family what he had as a child and more. But for the time being we lived in a stuffed house. In it resided Grandma and her baby boy Monte, Dad, Mom, me, Caren, Auntie Joycelyn, and her son, Jerry.

This living arrangement made us happy when it came to dinnertime. We would laugh, love, and play. Grandma would cook wonderful and tasty Southern meals that included fried chicken, meat loaf, fish, liver, greens, potatoes, corn, homemade biscuits, and Jell-O. The food was satisfying. Yet the ambiance was as thick as the Bisquick biscuits Grandma ritualistically baked.

The house was filled with such strong personalities and motivations. As kids, we were always jumping around and having fun. Dad and Mom were trying to maintain some kind of youthful love as they were entering their seventh year of marriage. Grandma was always practicing and singing church songs; she was in the church choir. Aunt Joycelyn, well, we did not see her much. She was enjoying life in her own way. While participating in many clubs and working full time, she was perpetually on the road. Uncle Monte was different. Some say he had sugar in his tank; others felt he just hung around girls too much. Either way, the familial and social situation of the Zathers and Carnegies warranted some adjustments. Someone had to go.

Auntie Joycelyn and Jerry moved first. Although, change in address didn't matter; Jerry was always over to Grandma's house anyway. Auntie Joycelyn was always traveling, working, networking with organizations that she was connected with, or just having fun, so Grandma or my mom always kept him. After school, we would congregate in Grandma's living room, waiting for our respective parents to get off work.

Dad worked at a rubber-making factory. Mom worked at a factory where they made cookware. Grandma had retired from her residence cleaning and retail jobs. Auntie Joycelyn had the most white-collar job. She worked in accounts payable at an international steel company. We weren't rich and we weren't poor. We made do with what we had. As far as I could see, we were doing all right. To this day people tell me we were poor, but my dad had a way of concealing the disenfranchised existence. He promoted kingly living.

One day Caren and Jerry, also known as busybodies, reasoned to steal money from Grandma's purse, go to the neighborhood store, and buy candy. Being the analytical, logical giant that God designed me to be, I sat and watched. Jeremiah 1:5 reads, "Before I formed you in the womb I knew you, before you were born I set you apart." I had no desire to steal or leave the house without asking permission.

I said, "Y'all gonna get it." That didn't matter to them. They left and came home from the store laughing, dancing, and licking. Grandma came in interrogating. "Where did ya get the money to buy that candy?" While Caren and Jerry scrambled to find the most innocent answer, I reserved myself while holding back unbearable laughter, to be the pompous, spoiled soul that I was unconsciously or consciously being trained to be.

Most times, the aforementioned traits are common traits of the firstborn child; one who is controlling, strong, and impenetrable. In my case, the assumption is true.

After much denial and fear, Caren and Jerry told the truth. Grandma whipped them with the warm heart of the leather strap and the acidic tone of her God-fearing tongue. In the end, I got all the candy that they had purchased.

That incident was the beginning to what I and the rest of the family to this day perceive as the reign of Princess Angel. I was innocent, pure, the oldest, and most importantly, supernaturally gifted by God. The magnitude of the ordination was priceless. Although I didn't know the effects of the gifting then, eventually I would not be able to deny it.

Amid our recalcitrant behaviors, inquisitive adventures, and subsequent spankings, Mom, Dad, and Auntie Joycelyn worked. We were a family, and love always prevailed. Mom would come home, assist Grandma in cooking, talk with us, and eagerly await Dad's return.

His return was always the unknown factor in the equation. We would inquire about where Dad was, when he was coming home, and how long he had to work today, but Mom never knew the answer. She would always assure us that he would return. Meanwhile, we would sing, pray, learn, recite Bible Scriptures, play, and wait together.

Mom was a deeply religious person. She learned that from her mother. Soon, she would grow on her own to have the personal relationship with God that he desires from all his children. She was constantly reading the Holy Bible and watching Christian television.

Mom made sure that we attended Sunday school, Vacation Bible School, morning worship, evening worship, you name it. Any event dealing with church, we were there. Mom's objective was two-pronged: to teach us the virtues and values of our Lord and Savior Jesus Christ and to pray deliverance for my dad. She would pray and speak in tongues. We would just laugh, all the while not knowing that there was a greater force in the mix of language that Mom uttered. These spiritual activities would predict the direction of the rest of the life of her children and her husband.

Chapter 2

While we worshipped God Almighty, Dad danced and partied with the gods of drugs, booze, fast times, and loose women. At the time, we didn't realize that kind of partying included partaking in illicit drugs, dating, and having sex with myriad women. But Mom knew, and that made her more determined to, as she put it, "Pray the devil out of your daddy." Eventually, Mom would recruit us to help pray the devil out of Dad.

Some say kids don't understand all that Jesus stuff, but Mom said we knew what to pray and how to pray. Psalm 8:2 reads: "From the lips of children and infants you have ordained praise because of your enemies, to silence the foe and the avenger." According to Mom, we had been recruited as ambassadors for Christ to rebuke the devil out of Dad's life. Our assignment, when fulfilled, would bring glory to the Kingdom of God.

In spite of the obvious dichotomy, spirit against flesh that existed in our family, Dad continued to work and provide for his family. Mom continued to work and pray, and we kids continued to go to school and pray. Although it was a monotonous existence, it was our family: the Carnegie clan. When Dad couldn't provide enough living sustenance (which was most times), he would seek help from my paternal grandpa, PaPa.

PaPa Lonnie was a truck driver. He comes from a long lineage of truck drivers. People often say the desire to drive a truck runs in our blood. We found that to be somewhat true because our family owns a trucking company in North Carolina. Additionally, PaPa, his brothers, my uncles, and Dad would even try their foot to the pedal as truck drivers. However, PaPa was the only one to make a forty-five-year career of it.

PaPa and his wife, my grandma, NaNa (Martha), had seven kids: Bonita, Lonnie II, Chandler, Richard, Josie, Jackie, and Preston. To me, it seemed that the Carnegie family line always thought they were better than the Zathers. When we needed financial help, instead of blaming Dad for his less than provisional aptitude, the Carnegies would murmur, "We told you not to marry that woman. We knew that she would only bring you down."

I guess they blamed Mom for Dad's carousing, boozing, and womanizing. Even though we had their blood running through us, because of Mom, they still made us feel isolated and inferior.

At family gatherings, consciously or not, my paternal aunties would make us feel like outsiders. My conclusion was based on the looks, tone of voice, and nonchalant way that the Carnegie family treated Mom. The verbal and nonverbal communication conveyed an ideology that expressed, "We are watching you, Celeste, and you better not mess up." The behavior may have only been meant for Mom, but I noticed it and felt it. I reasoned, "If you do it to my mom, you do it to me." Although I loved them, there was always an unspoken reservation.

Because of Dad's familial omnipotence, we would spend Christmas and Thanksgiving and other holidays with the Carnegie family. NaNa was the one who made sure that we all gathered together at her house in order to maintain the closeness and bonding that a family needs for survival. During these gatherings, we had the opportunity to really see what we were made of, the characteristics that marked the Carnegies as distinct.

People say we look like we have Indian and white in us. We all had long and wavy hair, and we were fair skinned, almost white, or with reddish brown skin. Therefore, their isolated and stereotypical assumption made sense.

Our familial background was vast; it included black, white, Indian, French, and German. You name it, we had it. Ironically, we had such strong genes that people in the city would conclude, "You must be a Carnegie."

The men in the family were tall and handsome, with fine hair, and the ladies in the family were fair-skinned, cute, and shapely. My uncles were ideal picks, and all married, just as my aunties. They were ideal picks because they were good looking. They had decent jobs yet were not college-educated. My aunties and uncles were truck drivers, telephone operators, factory workers, and day-care providers. In the 1970s, these kinds of jobs guaranteed secure living.

Sadly, we would lose Uncle Richard at age thirty-six. He had a heart attack. This would take a toll on everyone, especially my Dad, and since he was the baby of the family, everyone treated him as such with meticulous mothering and sensitive sistering. "You all make sure to keep an eye on Preston, our baby boy," would be their eternal request.

The story goes that when Uncle Richard was hospitalized, he died and came back to life. When he returned from the dead, he said, "Please let me go back and be with Jesus." He said it was the best. He said, "I want to die and stay with Jesus." This notion befuddled some but sparked Dad's interest about God. He started going to church and reading the Bible.

The praying and worshipping God encounters that Mom and the kids relentlessly practiced were slowly but surely being answered. Galatians 6:19 states, "Don't grow weary in well doing, for you will reap a reward if you faint not." We were in it for the long haul.

We were a good-looking family, and we knew it. Mom disliked this pious aspect of the Carnegie family, but she loved them, in God's way. Nonetheless, NaNa loved on us, and her affinity for Mom would blossom into a most desirable in-law relationship. As this relationship continued to grow, so did another: Dad and Judy.

Good ole Judy. This was Dad's new girlfriend. She was the one we knew about. Mom and Dad had separated—again. We would frequently go over to visit with Dad at his new pad, Judy's house. We would have to visit that ugly witch. We hated it. Oh, but she was so nice and sweet. Apparently Dad liked her. Caren and I would hear them having sex every time we went to visit. Oh what cacophony.

The dismal and immoral reality was hurtful to us. But we could do nothing. We loved our Dad, but he was still married to Mom. Although we knew what was going on was wrong and strange, we were only kids, so we had no choice but to go with the flow.

We told Mom about the sexual escapades, and she suggested that Dad should not have us around Judy; yet he persisted and prevailed.

Eventually, he either got bored with Judy or our prayers worked. Judy was gone, and Dad wooed Mom back, just as he did in the hula-hooping days. He had a way of doing this. His approach was like clockwork. Mom and Dad would separate; he would move out, get a girlfriend, dump that girl, and then woo Mom back. Ritualistic or sadistic, this tennis match was the kind of love they and we had grown accustomed to—in one day and out the next.

During one reunion, our third sibling, Tonya, was born. She was the middle child. Mom was working so hard outside the home in order to supplement Dad's meager income that she didn't have the time or energy to breastfeed Tonya. Because of that fact, we all would make fun of Tonya. "Mom didn't like you so much that she didn't even breastfeed you." That notion would socially and emotionally impact Tonya's future like one could never imagine. Some would even go as far as to say from birth Tonya was the most neglected of the seven siblings. Grandma Bennie babysat Tonya. Caren and I went to school, and Mom worked.

Dad worked and partied. Mom worked and prayed. Yet, Dad insisted that he was a changed man. Grandma Bennie told Mom to leave him. She said, "He'll never change." Mom insisted that God could do the impossible. She calmly stated, "With man this is impossible, but with God all things are possible" (Matt. 19:26). Mom was one woman who exercised her faith with supernatural endurance. Soon after Grandma's petition, Dad found us a new house and what we thought was a new start.

Our new dwelling was inhabited by Dad, Mom, Caren, Tonya, and me. The surroundings were great. This house would humorously be named "Junky Down Side Down Green House" because of its appearance and shape. But we had a spacious backyard and a neighborhood park across the street. A remarkable transformation was taking place within the Carnegie home. Dad was getting to know the Father that we so fervently prayed he would, and we were getting to know our earthly father who was supposed to nurture us in the admonition of Christ.

Dad began to go to church worship and relate the goodness of God to his many miserable and wretched friends. These friends liked to smoke marijuana, drink alcohol, and peruse the bar scene. Yet, the demons and devils were ever present trying to trick him and keep him in bondage. These spirits taunted my dad. Ephesians 6 verse 12 reads, For our struggle is not against flesh and blood, but against the rulers, against the authorities, against the powers of this dark world and against the spiritual forces of evil in the heavenly realms. The spirits include drugs, sex, idolatry, disobedience, and anything that is contrary to the will of the living God.

When Tonya, Caren, and I were three, six, and nine, Dad and his friends would allow us to taste the spirits that kept them occupied while they played chess, listened to music, and babysat us. During the free-for-all festivals on the home front, they would also smoke marijuana.

One day Mom came home from church and found us surrounded by spirits and smokes. All fire and brimstone broke loose. Sure, she was beautiful, dutiful, and purposeful, but don't push the wrong button. The after effect of her rage would be something one would undoubtedly regret. It was like a scene in a Lifetime movie.

Mom ferociously charged at my dad with a knife in hand and shouted, "How dare you do this in our house and around our children. I want all of you out of here, now."

Since Dad was subdued by the acidic nature of Mom's tongue and the sharpness of the knife, he knew not to oppose. Mom was already under a great deal of pressure. The strain was mainly guilt due to the fact that Mom was not allowed to go and help care for her ailing mother as she desired because Dad wouldn't let her. He simply wouldn't let her. There was no rhyme and no reason.

Grandma Bennie had just recently passed away after a long, tedious bout with cancer. She used to dip snuff. I vividly recall her keeping a can beside her all the time. She would take the can and spit in it. How gross. I never understood how a beautiful, meek woman could possess and maintain such a bad, nasty, and dirty habit.

The disease started in her esophagus and spread throughout the rest of her body. Although Mom's siblings indicted her because of her scarcity in assisting them in caring for their mom, they knew Dad had orchestrated the isolation.

Because of Mom's tirade, the men left in a hurry. We sat by in supreme shock and joy. We didn't like those dirty scoundrels anyway. Mom saved the day. Her necessary nagging about the in-home parties also contributed to the change in Dad's life and our family's future.

We all began to attend worship together. Miraculously, Dad became an ordained minister. The conversion was a joyful event. Although the transformation wasn't overnight, Dad's change came immediately. It was supernatural. The Zather and Carnegie families finally agreed on something. Our praying and weeping for Dad had finally paid off. "The effectual and fervent prayers of the righteous availeth much" according to James 5:16b.

The transition was heaven sent. Dad was going to church, preaching the word, and being filled with the Holy Spirit. Dad had been converted. He was realizing the Kingdom mandate commissioned to the ambassadors of the Kingdom of God. Mark 16:15 reads, "And he said unto them, Go ye into all the world, and preach the gospel to every creature." Dad was treating, raising, and indoctrinating us about the royalty of Christ for our lives and in our lives. Dad was on fire and possessed a zeal for the kingdom of God.

As time went on, Dad continued to work in a factory where he made enough money to send us to a private parochial school. God, Dad, and Mom believed we deserved the best, and we got the best. Our present situation was decent and in order. We were a happy family. We had love, togetherness, food, shelter, clothes, and some luxuries. Dad was staying home often and studying God's Word. But like Mom always recited apostle Paul's admonishment in 1 Thessalonians 5:17, to "Pray without ceasing."

One day while working in the factory, where Dad was in charge of cutting materials, he turned his attention away for a split second. The machine, still in motion, came down on his hand, and he suffered a severed right thumb. The detachment was severe, but doctors could have repaired it to some degree of functionality. Dad said, "Take it off completely." Doctors completely removed his thumb. Dad had to learn how to use a stub as his new thumb. Charismatic Dad made light of the situation, joked, jested, and jived about it. He even, by faith, asked God to grow him another thumb. The mustard seed of faith was now blossoming in his life.

After returning from the hospital, Dad took us on a family vacation with the money that he received from the accident. We traveled to Atlanta, Georgia, to visit with my maternal family. We knew that God was now in control, because Dad didn't too much care for Mom's family. The love of God prompted him to take us anyway.

My family who lived in the South was different. They were a Cherokee Indian, Mexican, and black mix. They believed in working, cooking, eating, loving, working, cooking, and eating. It seemed that they honored the latter two more than anything else. I get fat just thinking about their dining doctrine.

The daily schedule would be to wake around eight in the morning and have what seemed like a twenty-six-course meal consisting of bacon, ham, sausage, eggs, oatmeal, potatoes, pancakes, biscuits, cereal, toast, and many other breakfast items. Then we would visit or play on the family farm. They owned many acres of land and had pigs, horses, and cows.

Then about eleven in the morning it was time for lunch. "We just ate," would be our cry. Auntie would feed us more meats, vegetables, sandwiches, salads, cakes, and pies. We would then resume visits with our cousins and play in the fields. No sooner than the food would commence to digesting, auntie would announce, "Time for dinner."

Auntie would prepare fried chicken, ribs, turkey, pork chops, mashed potatoes, corn on the cob, sweet potatoes, and desserts. The southern style of eating was all too much for us northerners to handle. Although our family had gained some pounds, we had a good old-fashioned southern visit. It was a visit of peace, love, and kindness. Dad and Mom were getting along perfectly and were enjoying family.

During the visits to the farms, playing with our family's horses, and walking the red dusty roads of Georgia, Dad was invited to meet and preach for one of the most prominent pastors in the Atlanta area, Rev. Sutherland. Sutherland was fine looking and spiritually divine. We instantly loved him. He was actually an aged version of my father.

The difference was that he had one of the biggest churches in the Atlanta area, and he was rich. He had a big home, a Mercedes Benz, and expensive suits and shoes. He had the looks, the charm, and the anointing. Mom believed that Sutherland had something to do with Dad's character growth. Sutherland and Dad would develop a preacher-preacher's son relationship.

Over the years, they would travel to each other's hometown and preach the gospel at each other's church home, respectively. Dad idolized, fantasized, and dreamed about being like Sutherland. The scary yet amazing thing about it was that he could do it. He could have the mega-church, mansion, and luxury cars. Dad was a young, impressionable, and on-fire babe in the body of Christ, yet he was hungry for the Word of God and for souls to be saved. Matthew 6:33 implores, "Seek first the Kingdom of God and his righteousness, and all these things will be added unto you." God's Word is true.

Sutherland was a mature, seasoned member of the body of Christ. This partnership in Christ would have its positives and pitfalls, but ultimately the goal still managed to be, in the grand scheme of things, about the Kingdom. They were fulfilling the great commission as ordained by Jesus in Matthew 28:18–20. It reads: "Then Jesus came to them and said, all authority in heaven and on earth has been given to me. Therefore go and make disciples of all nations, baptizing them in the name of the Father and of the Son and of the Holy Spirit, and teaching them to obey everything I have commanded you. And surely I am with you always, to the very end of the age."

Whether it was a weekly revival in Cambridge or Atlanta, souls by the hundreds were being saved and delivered from the grasp of the enemy. Dad and Sutherland preached the gospel of Christ with truth and conviction. With the revivals came long nights at church, much prayer and fasting, and a grandiose financial payday.

The spiritual consecration and victory in the number of souls that were added to the Lamb's book of life was good for the Kingdom. Moreover, the money raised to pay alms to the men of God was a special welcome for a man who had quit his job and gone into the ministry full time. Dad had dedicated his life to the fulfillment of his God-ordained assignment.

Deuteronomy 8:18 reads, "But remember the Lord your God, for it is he who gives you the ability to produce wealth …" Dad was being rewarded for his obedience to the Kingdom. Preaching was the gift given to him by God, and he was giving it back to God by way of preaching the gospel to the people.

CHAPTER 3

Dad continued to convey the message of Christ to the masses. Whenever he received an invitation to preach, he took it. Throughout this time he would comment that there was still something missing in his life. He was saved, and he had a faithful wife and three beautiful daughters; now he yearned for a son.

He reasoned with God, "I need a son. If you bless me with a son, I will forever preach your Word." Ecclesiastes 5:4–5 reads, "When you make a vow to God, do not delay in fulfilling it. He has no pleasure in fools; fulfill your vow. It is better not to vow than to make a vow and not fulfill it."

A year later was the birth of Dad's first son, Preston II, and the Discipleship Missionary Church. The church motto was, "To preach deliverance to the captives" (Luke 4:18).

One can only imagine the delight, happiness, and supreme magnificence that Mom realized when her husband was delivered from the hands of Satan and his imps. The prayers we petitioned to God were answered and exceedingly surpassed. God said the he would do immeasurably above all that we could ask or think. The Carnegie union was blessed, beautiful, and bound for success. As the natural family grew, Dad's desire for a spiritual family also grew.

Dad opened his own church. It was a storefront church located in a plaza in the section of town equally inhabited by blacks and whites. On one side of the building was a convenient store, on the other there was sometimes a realtor's office and sometimes a secondhand shop. Discipleship Missionary Church was sandwiched in the middle. Dad was young, charismatic, smooth, and saved. He knew the streets, but most importantly he knew the Savior. He appealed to the youthful and vibrant of the city. Ninety percent of the church was aged forty and under.

Initially, the membership consisted of my patriarchal family members: Dad's parents, brothers, sisters, aunts, uncles, nephews, nieces, cousins, and friends. Mom's family, still somewhat reserved, decided to stay with their home church. That didn't matter. Word got around that we worshipped, rejoiced, and praised the name of the living Savior. Interest was sparked, and growth in members was manifested.

Parishioners by the multitudes left their churches to become members of the new church on the block. Unbelievers from the streets were being compelled to come in and be saved. After all, who could turn down the Word of God being preached by a good-looking, trustworthy man of God who was anointed to preach deliverance to the captives? He knew it, we knew it, and the members knew it. The church membership grew from seven members to over two hundred in just over a year. In the early '80s this was a phenomenal feat.

Everything was ideal. We loved going to church. The union was strong. The bond was powerful. Since Dad had abandoned his job at the factory to become a full-time minister, we went back to public school.

16

Mom was a stay-at-home mom and maintained the house. She was in her bliss. She was proud of her husband and his new relationship with Christ. Mom enjoyed being a stay-at-home mom. The role gave her satisfaction. She was available for us, Dad, and the church. Although with four kids at times it was a struggle, she would recite Philippians 4:13, "I can do all things through Christ which strengthens me."

Throughout all the singing, preaching, and worshipping came the birth of Felicia, and a year later Grover. Felicia would grow up to be the tall, thin, prissy one, indifferent and almost just there. Grover, the second son, would be just that, "the second son." He would always long for a great connection, yet the vow Dad made seemed to have rested on the first son, Preston II. Even still, Mom would continue to impart the Word to all of us, and our futures would be immensely blessed.

The saying goes, parents have their favorite child. Although Dad had his first son, I was, and noticeably so, his favorite. Mom, I believe, tried to love us all the same. How could you not? There were so many of us, back to back. The kids kept coming. But above all, we were a complete family of beauty and balance. Symmetry—we had it, we shared it, and we represented it.

Church members and people in the city always said, "That Rev. Carnegie has a beautiful family and with all those little kids." We had made it. We were a paragon of familial greatness that other families in the black community emulated and prayed to be like.

Dad's only pastoral income was fifty dollars a week, and with the supplement of government help and preaching engagements, it was still hard to make a living. Yet, my parents still tithed 10 percent of their income. Sometimes we kids didn't understand. Dad was taking money out of the home when at times we didn't have food to eat. But as Mom always put it, "God will provide." That he did. We had the greatest of these: love. We managed to have food, shelter, a car, clothes, and candies.

Dad always made us happy by bringing home snacks. We would always ask, "Dad, did you bring home any snacks?" It was the completion of our day to hear Dad drive up, turn the key, open the door, and walk in the house with a brown paper bag loaded with Snider's chips, candy, and soda pop. As we devoured the once-a-week treats, we would talk about our day at school and church-related activities, play games, or just spend time together. The ritual was divine. We loved it. We loved him. He was our man, our protection, and our provider.

With the astronomical growth in the church, time spent with Dad began to dissipate. We would see him right after school for dinner, and then he would have to hurry to Bible study, prayer meeting, a trustee or deacon meeting, or choir rehearsal; there was always something related to church. He would then return around nine o'clock each evening right before we were dismissed to bed. Mom would do her best to satisfy and sustain all six of us until Dad would return.

At first the time away from home was understandable, but soon the return time of nine o'clock turned to eleven and then twelve. Dad's rationale was always, "We had a meeting over dinner at a restaurant in town," or "I counseled someone at church." Nonetheless, with us going to church almost as much as Dad for various extra-curricular activities, the time spent away still managed to appear acceptable.

Within the year, we resided in a new government housing development in a majority white neighborhood. Our new single-family home was big enough for a family of eight. The house had four bedrooms, two full baths, a basement, a spacious kitchen and dining area, an office for Dad, and a plentiful front and backyard for us kids. At home, we would play church, and my brothers, especially Preston II, would preach. The rest of us would pretend to be the choir.

Mom, at times, would even play along and pray with us, but especially for us because she knew the ultimate effect the repetition of the Word, whether for play or real, would have on us. The Holy Bible in Joshua 1:8 says, "Do not let this Book of the law depart from your mouth; meditate on the word day and night …" With us playing church at home and almost living at the church, the saturation of the Word in our spirit was inevitable.

We played a lot, indoors and out. We would spend endless hours outside playing hide and seek, grown up, church, kickball, school, you name it. What I liked best was the fact that I was always in charge. I was the oldest. What we would play and how we would play was my call.

But one day Grandma, the name we affectionately began to call my sister Tonya because she acted so old-fashioned, wanted to do something else. Ms. Non-Breastfed Tonya wanted to play a different game. I said no. Because she couldn't get her way, she ran into the house and locked us out. Tonya had begun to exhibit some signs that made us question, "Is she really related to us?" The relationship was hard to explain, but maybe that breastfeeding event, or lack thereof, is more important to kids than parents and pediatricians really realize.

Mom and Dad were gone. Princess Angel was in charge. Caren, Preston II, Felicia, Grover, and I started banging on the door with shoes, sticks, anything that would convince "Grandma" that we meant business. "Let us in," we shouted. Finally, I gave the day of reckoning bang; it broke the glass block out of the window that was located in the side door. Then Grandma let us in, all right. The kids started crying and yelling.

Mom and Dad pulled up after a not-so-frequent yet relished night out. Dad questioned, "What happened, Angel?" Even though it was my final bang to the glass block that broke the window and I was the culprit, I blamed all the other kids. They said, "No, Dad, Angel did it." But he clandestinely surmised, "Not my princess."

The clan got a spanking. One after the other, Dad issued a leather lashing. I sat back and laughed. Wrong though I was, I was also the princess. Afterward Mom said she would stay home more often because the job of babysitting was getting to be too much for me to handle. Once again Dad was off to do his kingdom assignment, but now he was on his own, with no Mommy and no Carnegie clan.

Dad began to have more meetings, counseling sessions, and the like. We also started to receive more guests at our home. Myriad ladies from the church started to come over, bearing gifts of food, goodies, clothes, and offers of help with cleaning or to give Mom a break from watching kids. On the surface, the gestures appeared acceptable and normal. Never forget what the Bible says—the devil will come as a beacon of light, but beware. However, I didn't understand the caution when I was twelve.

Over time Dad began to be called upon to preach revivals. This type of calling would require him to travel to many cities around the country, exhorting the Word of God. He would travel to Atlanta, St. Louis, Baltimore, and cities in California, Virginia, and North Carolina. Dad would be gone for a week at a time. Once or twice Mom would accompany him, but that soon came to a halt. Whether because of us or the quickly fabricated arguments Mom and Dad would have, she would conveniently decide to stay home.

Whatever the case, according to the Bible, Mom understood that Dad was doing the work of her Father, Jesus, so she never once complained. In the grand scheme of things, that's all that matters, right? Mark 16:15 reads, "Go into all the world and preach the good news to all creation."

If Mom said the activity was fine, it must be. Dad's travels became especially fine, fun, and fantastic to me. I was given the opportunity and privilege to travel with Dad to Atlanta. Daddy's little girl, his spitting image, Princess Angel, went to a preaching engagement in Atlanta. We were off via airplane to Reverend Sutherland's church. At Dad's previous visit, he met the Douglass family. They had a daughter about my age, and in her I met a friend for life.

Throughout the years, she would visit me and I would visit her. We became traveling pen pals. She would become a confidante and a support system that I value to this day. During our visit, I stayed with the Douglass family, who also attended Reverend Sutherland's church.

The Douglasses lived in a big, beautiful home. Boy did I long to one day have a home like theirs. Her father was an established businessman and her mother an accomplished insurance provider. Simply put, "They had it going on."

The Douglasses had nice, fashionable clothes, good name brand food, and flashy cars. I wanted that. Dad wanted that. And if anyone could get us there, it would be Dad. In my mind, we were almost there. Based on kingdom mandate, we were royalty and we deserved a prosperous living.

According to the Word of God, we are a chosen generation, a royal priesthood. And Dad treated us like royalty. He understood the principles of the Kingdom of God. One would call our home and the answering machine message would state, "You have reached the Carnegie kingdom. The kings and queens are not available. Please leave a message." He said it, we believed, Mom and Dad taught it, and God confirmed it. We were on our way to acquiring the finer things in life.

Once, the week of revival had expired, and Dad would make what appeared to me (Dad would let us see and at times let us help count the cold cash) a tax-free couple grand for his services. Then my best and only boyfriend and I would return back to Cambridge. Dad always said, "I am your only boyfriend, until you turn thirty." (Oddly enough, I would marry at age thirty.) I welcomed that notion in my formal years. After all, Dad was my hero, my provider, and my protector.

As I began to grow and mature, the fondness, respect, and rapport that we once shared somehow became a distortion to my reality. And by the age of twelve, that pristine, unspoiled relationship was challenged. Angel, the princess, was losing her position, mansion, horse, and carriage to … *she.*

She was the sharp, sophisticated, smart-dressing, and young junior church usher board director. *She* was a divorced mother with one son. *She* worked as an administrative assistant for a battered women's shelter.

All the kids liked her. *She* would bring snacks to church meetings and compliment our every move. *She* appreciated all the youth. *She* was energetic and purposeful. However, *she* liked Caren and me best. We looked at her like she had a good life: money, youth, and nice, stylish clothes. *She* wasn't attractive in her face but she attracted attention because of her poise and style of dress. *She* was at church every Sunday morning, serving, adhering to everything the *reverend* (my dad) said.

The season had come to get new usher uniforms for church. *She* chose Caren and me to go along for the ride. While on our fashion trip, *she* talked of how well mannered we were and how much she liked our dad. *She* enjoyed how he preached, his style of dress, and how he sincerely catered to the young people. *She* perpetually and poignantly talked about him. The soliloquy was too much for my standard of like and respect. *She* was too impressed by and with my dad. Even my nine-year-old sister noticed it. Caren, from the backseat of the car, discretely, secretly, coyly tapped my arm, as if to say, "What is the deal? Why does she keep talking about Dad?"

It was as if *she* was in fairytale land and was envisioning a plan of togetherness of her and our dad as a complete family, which suited her reality. From that day forward, I watched, wondered, and waited to see just how much *she* really liked my Dad. *She* was Aubrey.

CHAPTER 4

It was time, Dad said, to move into our new church building. We had
the membership, the money, the popularity, and most importantly,
the faith. And with these assets we moved, and God moved mountains.
"For verily I say unto you, That whosoever shall say unto this mountain,
Be thou removed, and be thou cast into the sea; and shall not doubt in
his heart, but shall believe that those things which he saith shall come
to pass; he shall have whatsoever he saith" (Mark 11:23). We had faith,
and we moved.

We moved into a seven hundred–seat church once inhabited by
an apostolic congregation. They had three morning services, with
a membership of two thousand. They moved into a bigger, more
accommodating church home, and we moved into our blessing. We
were now big time.

We took our three hundred members, and on a Sunday, with a
caravan of at least what look like a thousand cars by a kid's standard,
we moved to the other side of town to our new place of worship. Our

new church neighborhood was centered amid what some perceived as the ghetto. There were black people, and then there were those who society would label as poor white trash. But the church stood out as the White House in Harlem. We were blessed and proud. God is in the real fast blessing business. He is the same yesterday, today, and forevermore. After only a couple of years, we had moved from a storefront church existence to a free-standing, grandiose place of worship.

Dad was on the right track doing what Dad vowed he would do for God for the rest of his life—win souls to Christ. We had the faithful members from the neighborhood where we had traveled from the old storefront community. With that God added new members from the present community. The membership was a new mix of the old youth with the new youth. We still rocked and rolled to God's name. We began to travel across the state from Athens to Cleves, to Lorain, and to Yorktown. We experienced and worshipped with different churches all over the east coast.

Our Sunday was filled with church services from 9:00 a.m. to 9:00 p.m. The communal sentiment was that no one got tired. The church was always a full house, and no one complained. If reverend said it was so, it was. It was like Dad had become the Jim Jones of Cambridge. The members were under his direction. Whatever he desired, the church would do their best to accommodate him and to fulfill the Kingdom mandate that he so articulately and passionately proclaimed.

Truly, it was amazing how the church members were so motivated and captivated to please Dad. Oh yeah, they loved and worshipped God, but Dad, filled with the Holy Spirit, was enthralling them beyond belief. He was preaching the good news to the people.

As the church membership grew, so did Sunday offerings and thusly Dad's income. Our family was starting to enjoy the fruits of his labor.

We had all gone to see a Saturday movie matinee. We were a family, Dad, Mom, and the kids. The flick was a good and wholesome family movie. We all cried at the end, all except for Dad, of course. On the way home, we took a detour from our normal route. And we, unknowingly, found another piece to the puzzle of our royal life.

It sat atop a hill, in a pristine, all-white neighborhood (except for one black family). The house had a two-car garage, large, fenced-in backyard, five bedrooms, one full bath and two half baths, two fireplaces, office space, a basement, a family room, and a dishwasher, and it was made for us. Dad looked at Mom, and they said, "This is it." He did it again. And within the next six months, we were nestled into our very own home.

Through the years we, that I can remember, had lived with Grandma, Auntie Joyce, black folks, and white folks, and now we lived with each other in our own home. The procurement of our new house really proved that Dad was the victor, the best, and could do anything he said he could.

The Carnegie family always said he would be someone great. Aunt Josie said, "Your dad was on *Soul Train* as a dancer and wore everybody out. He was destined for greatness, beginning at a young age." And as we could tell, there was nothing else for him to be. The supernatural and kingly attributes all came so naturally. Now he was dancing for God.

First Peter 2:9 states, "But you are a chosen people, a royal priesthood, a holy nation, a people belonging to God, that you may declare the praises of him who called you out of darkness into his wonderful light." Not surprisingly that year, we won the City League Family of the Year award. Love and faith had brought us to this season of our life. I am reminded of the blessings for obedience captured in Deuteronomy 28. In summary, it reads: "You will be blessed in the city and blessed in the country … You will be blessed when you come in and blessed when you go out … The Lord will make you the head and not the tail …" Conversely, and understandably, within this chapter there are also curses listed for disobedience.

With our many church travels in state, our church family finally got the opportunity to leave the state. Discipleship Church was invited to a church in North Carolina. The invitation came from a minister friend of my father's who used to have a church in Massiton, Indiana. The minister had now relocated to the Carolinas. Good ole Rev. Pruitt. He was, as some would say, my dad's best buddy.

Pruitt was college educated, as were many members of his church. He spoke with the most bombastic vernacular I had ever witnessed in any church. Mom said it was because the church was of the AME denomination, African Methodist Episcopal. This denomination was noted for being poised, structured, and regimented in worship and lifestyle.

Why and how he spoke, lived, and operated so well didn't matter to me. I just wanted to communicate like the Rev. Pruitt. No matter how long I needed to practice or train, I was willing to make the sacrifice. (It's amazing who and what shapes one's adulthood.) His tone exuded a British accent and smooth, accurate speech. His wife was a schoolteacher. They didn't have any kids. They appeared to be sophisticated nerds, but it looked so uppity, so pure, and so graceful, yet innocent. I wanted to be just like them. Dad, along with the entire church, went to Pruitt's church in Charlotte for a Sunday worship service.

The service would be a kick-off program for a weeklong revival. Discipleship Church had a chartered a bus. Some members drove their own cars, and a handful rode in the plane with Dad. Mom, the kids, and I rode on the bus. Aubrey and her mother were among the handful of people who traveled by plane with Dad.

There were whispers about the strange travel arrangements and how suspect the behavior was. Even Dad's secretary, whom we all thought had something going on with Dad, pointed to and questioned the obvious. "Why didn't your mom get to ride on the plane with your dad? How strange is that?"

Surely the reason wasn't because of us kids. We could have been babysat by relatives who rode the bus, or we also could have traversed on the plane with Mom and Dad.

To add spice to the gumbo, or make matters more suspicious, when we boarded the bus to leave and return to Cambridge on Sunday evening, Aubrey and her mother stayed in Charlotte for a couple more weeks. Are you serious?

One of my good friends, Molly, who, along with her parents and siblings, was a member of the church, and if I couldn't go somewhere neither could she, inquired, "Why didn't your mom stay with your dad and ride in the plane?" The scenario was like she was being raised by my father. Molly's mother would say, "If Reverend says it's all right for Angel to go, then you can go." I remember most vividly the NAACP was hosting a youth concert at the City League, and everyone my age was going to be there. There would be security, protection, guards, you name it.

But Dad said I could not go. He didn't want me to get hurt, or the boys to bother me. I did not get to go, Molly, to my surprise, did. I cried the entire night.

When I awoke, my eyes were puffy and red, as if I had been beaten up. To make circumstances worse, I had to read the morning announcements at church in front of the entire congregation. I found myself in a terrible situation. Before we left the house for morning worship, Dad commented, "If I knew you wanted to go that bad, I would have let you go." I murmured, "Yeah, right." Molly came to church and just bragged about the concert.

In her conversation she stated how she had been having so much fun over the summer—first Charlotte, North Carolina, and now the biggest concert in Cambridge. Oh yeah, she also quivered, "Why didn't your mom ride on the plane, but Aubrey did? Also Aubrey and her mother stayed an additional week after the revival." Why was Molly rubbing salt in an unattended to wound? I wondered the same thing. The behavior sparked my interest. I was on a mission to find out what was going on. Was Aubrey trying to take my dad away from Mom, the family, the church, God, and me?

Dad returned from the revival in Charlotte, and we proceeded with life as normal. Dad was at church and Mom at home (now enrolled in college), still managing the house and kids. Mom had taken on more responsibility, and so had I.

I am just like Dad in a lot of ways, so I'm told. I am spoiled like him, stubborn like him, look like him, have a temper like him, want to control like him, and am analytical like him. So I took it upon my obstinate, analytical self to review the family phone bill. If you are blessed with spiritual discernment, then you know why I was prompted to do such a thing at such a young age. This particular phone bill itemized the previous month's calls from the month of the spirit-filled revival in Charlotte.

The week following Dad's return home, there were countless phone calls to Charlotte from Cambridge. Dad and Rev. Pruitt are good friends, but it wasn't his phone number. I called the number. Aubrey answered. I hung up. I, being startled yet perturbed, immediately showed Mom. In showing Mom, I also expressed how Aubrey talked about Dad all the time, looked at him, and stayed the extra week in Charlotte.

Mom snapped, "Angel, you had no right to investigate and indict your dad, and don't let me hear you say anything like that about your dad again." Within her admonition, I also heard sadness, suspicion, and despair. Mom now suspected, or probably already knew, something was going on between Dad and Aubrey.

This consternation would soon be physically, emotionally, and mentally realized. I was sad, hurt, and furious. I knew that I was onto something indictable, but I didn't have the evidence or support that I needed to further investigate. I wanted to know. Was Dad committing adultery? If the allegation was true, it was wrong. After all, Dad preached against this iniquity regularly in his Sunday-morning sermons. The Bible said it was wrong. And on TV, those who participated in it were always punished. Right?

I remember JR on the television drama series *Dallas*. He was always suffering due to the consequences of his adulterous lifestyle. JR was socially alienated by his son, shot by a mistress, or lost his powerful position due to his involvement in precarious behaviors.

Dallas was one of the family's favorite shows to watch on Friday. If there was a revival going on, we would rush home from church, and wonder, "Who shot JR? Who shot Bobby Ewing?" Just as on TV, we witnessed corruption (except for the shooting, although there was an occasion when a female member of the church tried to stab Dad with a butter knife), adultery, and sin, all with the permission of our parents. But now the lights, camera, action were being illuminated on our family. We wondered, "Is Dad messing around or not?"

Thou shalt not commit adultery. The principle is one of God's Ten Commandments. Therefore, I needed to know the truth. Was the man I admired, respected, and worshipped involved in one of the most reprehensible acts against self, spouse, and Savior? I sat back, continued to take notes, and waited.

Growing up in the church, I was always taught that if you reflect, ask God, and wait, it—whatever you are in search of—will be revealed to you. And wouldn't you know it, over time the affair between Aubrey and Dad would became as clear as the morning sun.

Dad began to stay out for unspeakable hours into the night— unspeakable, at least, for a married father, not to mention a preacher of the gospel. Moreover, he became unbearably rude to Mom. "You eat too much. You don't keep the house clean. Your cooking is bad. You're slow," became the tyrannical cacophony that Dad would spew at Mom on a daily basis. And when he was home, he would stay confined to his office, leaving us to wonder, "Have we done something wrong?"

The happy-go-lucky provider became the unwelcome ole alienator. During this tumult, I noticed Mom reverting back to the times and the things that she used to do before Dad became saved. She would pray without ceasing, speak in tongues, cry, and plead the blood of Jesus.

Throughout, Aubrey became more visible in the church. When she wasn't ushering, she would sit two pews directly behind my mom, who sat right behind Dad. She was in our lives and on our phone. She began to call and hang up if Dad didn't answer the phone. What nerve! Aubrey was determined to get Dad and stay with him no matter what.

I can recall one time Mom needed some money from Dad to go to the grocery store. He told us to come to the church, which had now become his first home, to pick up the money. When we arrived, we saw Aubrey walking out. She looked disheveled. Her lipstick was smeared, as if something or someone had made it evaporate, and she looked shocked as if she thought, *I was planning on being gone before you all got here.* There were no other cars at the church, no one else, only Dad and Aubrey. Aubrey looked like she had seen an apparition. In my sibling and my eyes, they were busted.

Caren ran past her to get to Dad and retrieve the money. Mom told Aubrey hello, and she replied with the same return salutation. I may be young, but I knew when someone looked guilty, and it wasn't Mom. As we drove away, I immediately said to Mom, "Why was she there? Was anyone else there? What did Dad say?" I got no response.

All the actions of Dad and Aubrey were questionable yet unsubstantiated up to that point, and this just made it more suspicious. Throughout the skepticism, Mom continued to be optimistic. "Just continue to pray for your Dad," she would implore.

Although the suspicions resounded, the babies kept coming. Baby girl Katie, the last of the Preston and Celeste Carnegie clan, was born. Katie would become the second most spoiled. Everyone loved her and showered her with an abundance of love and attention, just as they had done to me. The oldest and the youngest kids, both female, looked alike, were spoiled, and as time would reveal, felt the same toward their number-one boyfriend, Dad.

CHAPTER 5

L ife became living. We were living for the moment. We would go to school, go to church, and deal with the pressures of being a pastor's kid and a pastor's family. Kids in school would make fun of us. By this time we were on community TV programming. Our family became quite visible. Dad would preach with fervency and zeal. He conveyed a redemptive word, but to the unlearned the delivery was entertaining. Amid all the now-alleged affairs with other women and other issues, like Dad's business, the church still continued to prosper. And with that prosperity came more responsibility, exposure, rumors, and hours away from home.

Dad became the new TV minister. This newfound celebrity would begin to somewhat overshadow the suspected infidelity with Aubrey. Our church was televised once a week as Dad continued his task of preaching deliverance to the captives. With the visibility, some would voice, "Here comes a big head, Dad's." His behaviors began to confirm the infamous Carnegie's identity of pomposity and invincibility.

Although he felt that our life was balanced, I witnessed the strain in the marriage, children, and church family. Dad didn't question anything or anybody, and he didn't let anyone question him. He had work to do in spite of the innuendos that he was having a multitude of extramarital affairs. Some even alleged that he fathered children outside his marriage to Mom. The latter could only be rumor since Dad had the physical attribute that granted men the ability to have kids surgically taken care of right after my baby sister Katie was born.

The kids at school would slyly question, "Is that your dad I see preaching and whooping on TV for Jesus? Isn't your dad the player, the pimp? Doesn't he have a lot of girlfriends?" I, in embarrassment, would say, "No." But they knew he was my dad. We have strong genes. I felt like Peter when he denied knowing Jesus. I couldn't help it. I felt like a social pariah. No one else I knew had parents who were as outspoken for Christ and the black community as was my father. And no one else had a father who was being mean to their mother and being accused, rightly so, of having myriad affairs. What a heavy load to carry. By kid standards, it was rough being a PK, preacher's kid.

As if we didn't have enough to deal with growing up with fame and alleged affairs, we found out that we had another sister. We have a half-sister named Shawnee.

She was conceived years ago while Dad was in the Air Force, stationed in Colorado. She was born ten months before my sister Caren. Shawnee, like Aubrey, had been kept a secret. Shawnee's mother told her that Dad was dead. She told Dad that he was forever out of their life. But like the old saying goes, "What's done in dark is sure to come to the light."

I would soon find out Mom already knew. But all was forgotten, by the command of Dad. That memory lapse lapsed when I turned fifteen. Mom planned a barbecue for the big event. The ceremony was the introduction of our new almost-grown half-sister.

Aunts, uncles, and friends came over. The fanfare was fun. We thought the introduction was cool and welcomed Shawnee with open arms; after all, the meeting was only a one-day visit. But the following year that one-day holiday turned into a permanent relocation. Rumor had it that Shawnee wasn't getting along with her mother and step-father. Shawnee moved from a home in Colorado, a home she shared with her mother, step-father, and sister, to a home she would now share with a father she did not know, his wife, and seven kids.

The familial addition was a dramatic transition. Mom, being the precious, God-fearing woman that she was born to be, made it as smooth as possible for everybody involved. Albeit difficult, we all tried to cope—we meaning Mom and the kids. Dad was so busy and inundated with the church and other extracurricular activities that he didn't realize that his family was being torn apart by an invisible, uninvited evil force. The Satan that we had prayed out of Dad years prior had resurfaced but as an indescribable, unnoticed, yet ugly power.

As a family, we had to adjust in school, church, community, and neighborhood, wherever we had ties and interaction. Remember, we had won the family of the year award, and God was on our side. So now what was really going on?

Shawnee was on the scene, settling in. Everyone in our circle was saying that we looked alike. "Your family has some strong genes." Yet, Shawnee was so much lighter, almost white. I called her glow worm. She hated it. Questions, thoughts, and reservations about her heritage began and did not relent. The situation started to become more and more of a thorn in our side than an addition to the family tree.

The community looked at the state of affairs as most of the family did. "How could a man of God with a beautiful wife and family have an outside daughter that no one knew existed with another woman?" These comments came despite the fact that the affair happened while Dad was young and years before he met Jesus as his personal Savior. The community could not shirk the evil that lurked in the church, the alleged affairs, and as we would come to find out about, the other women, Pam, Jackie, and Debbie, that Dad was allegedly sleeping with. The reality just didn't make logical, justified sense.

Meanwhile, my siblings and I began to see all the confusion and turmoil take a toll on Mom. Here was a woman who supported, aided, and stood by her husband before and throughout his spiritual birth and maturation to the pinnacle of pulpits. She birthed his children, cooked his food, and kept his home. However, she realized that she wasn't getting the love that God purposed for the wife from her husband.

Ephesians 5:25–27 reads, "Husbands, love your wives, just as Christ loved the church and gave himself up for her to make her holy, cleansing her by the washing with water through the word, and to present her to himself as a radiant church, without stain or wrinkle or any other blemish, but holy and blameless." I guess Dad neglected to read these verses about unity between husband and wife.

Mom began to question Dad. He would just blow her off with recitation of this infamous statement, "What are you complaining about? You have a home, car, and clothes. What more do you want?"

Mom's mother was dead, and other than God, my paternal grandmother, NaNa was the only person Mom could talk to. NaNa would soothe and comfort and tell Mom everything would be all right. She was so assured and confident in her affirmation. Unknown to Mom, but NaNa had been dealing with PaPa cheating, scheming, and lying for many years.

After much or little assuaging, Mom would fold. She would always regress to the fact that she never had a dad due to the shooting and untimely death of her own father. She didn't want us to experience the indescribable void. She decided to stay with Dad in spite of the infidelity or disrespect. And that she did.

Mom continued to cook, care, and pray for my Dad. I did not understand the motivation. Yeah, I still loved him, but I despised his actions. All the while, I would discuss the disdain with my siblings, all except his daughter, Shawnee. She was also starting to get on my nerves. She wanted attention. She looked different. She acted different. She thought different. We were raised differently from her. By this time, there were three people to blame for Mom's, or should I say my, unhappiness: Dad, Shawnee, and Aubrey.

Being the oldest, I had to continue to try and make sense of the dilemma for everyone: Mom, the kids, the church family, and anyone who would have the nerve to ask me. I was looked upon as mature and grown up, Rev. Preston's little princess who could handle anything. But all the while I was being tested, tried, and put to the task. Who was going to be my solace and my refuge?

In school my friends would say, "Your sister is nice but different." She never really fit in. We were family of the year. She grew up in a broken home. Little did I know our familial circumstances were just as out of order as her ancestral experiences. Neither my classmates nor Shawnee understood that we were reared in entirely different backgrounds and for both parties the "We are family concept" would be a hard transition to foster.

With the added strain of trying to include her, I began to despise her, and I expressed this discomfort with my siblings. Caren, Tonya, Preston II, Grover, and Felicia (Katie was just a toddler) would always go along with what I said. Like Dad, I had power. But Mom would say, "Angel, you have to learn how to get along. This is your sister." I did not care, and with Mom's earnest request, I thought even she was against me.

By this time the stress was so thick one could compare it to the distance that I wished Shawnee would travel back to Colorado. Throughout Dad was either confused or in denial. He was not questioned or even confronted with the antagonism being experienced in the Carnegie home. He always kept himself occupied with church business or other people's business. When he would come home, he would just lock himself in his office, work on the computer, watch TV, read the Bible, and smoke cigarettes. We hated the smell of cigarettes. Mom would implore Dad to smoke in the garage. But he thought keeping the door of his office closed would eliminate the terror caused by the cancerous fumes. He was busy. Mom was stressed. The clan was in turn left to fend for ourselves.

I pride myself on looking nice. I was considered one of the best-dressed students in the high school. I didn't like anyone of my siblings to wear my clothes, and everyone knew it. Usually Shawnee and I would ride the same bus to school, but this particular day she waited for a later bus. I asked why, and she said, "I am not ready yet."

So I went on to school. Around third period, a good friend of mine commented, "Your sister looks nice in your sweater."

I angrily said, "Which one?"

He responded, "Your favorite royal blue one."

I hunted for her, and when I found her, it was on. I said, "You little sneak. Don't you ever wear my clothes again." Anything and everything she did irritated me.

Thank goodness she had another shirt underneath the sweater, because I made her take my sweater off right there on the spot.

Call me what you might, but I perceived her as adding imbalance to what I perceived as my once-perfect family. I was mature, but I was also selfish and controlling. My life was unraveling around me. Was I born this way or was I groomed this way? Being Dad's favorite and clone was becoming challenging. Since I was also feeding Mom the details of Dad's suspected affairs and playing the role of the middle person with respect to the new addition of the family, the assignment to control the situation was almost unbearable.

I could not help but be in the middle of everything. Sure, I was only in high school, but I was the oldest sibling. I had been groomed, even though spoiled, to be alert, grown up, perfect, and knowledgeable.

The pressure was on. The whole family started to feel angst and anxiety. Dad and I would go for weeks without speaking to one another. Since I was so much like him, the attitude was understandable and mutual.

But I always had to be the one to give in and resume conversation first since I needed him for money. He was the only one in the house working. And boy would he rub that dominance in. After and during the request for money, Dad would give me the longest, driest, most unnecessary, so I thought, lecture. "Who do you think you are to go around my house, eat my food, and not talk to me? You better remember what side your bread is buttered. I provide for you." He thrived off that premise. And it was true. I learned early on that I needed to get a job so I could purchase my own food and take care of myself, and that I did. Dad and I would eventually mend the blanket, but our relationship still remained cold. He knew I was on to him. He groomed me, so why was he mad?

As far as I could tell, Dad would continue to ignore any hint of familial debate or confrontation, except when Shawnee voiced her desire to return home to Colorado. I was granted my wish. My half sister was exiled. I was conveniently blamed by my siblings for Shawnee's departure. "Look what you've done, Angel. You told her to go home." Although

I adamantly denied it, deep down I felt sorry for her predicament. Shawnee had been abused, alienated, and left alone. But in a way so had we.

The quandary was a terrible situation. And once again I had to explain to all those I had previously told about the addition to the family why it was no longer so. We were confused. The family tree was being uprooted.

People would wonder what was going on up there on the hill. It was like an epidemic spreading around. "Rev. Carnegie is sleeping with this person, taking the church's money, and keeping company with malefactors." Albeit some of them alleged, indictments and innuendos were predictable and as common as a Sunday morning service.

Mom would tell me, "Don't let it get you down. It's just that ole devil trying to destroy the family again. And I wouldn't let that disgusting demon have my family." Talk about mustard seed faith. In the face of obvious adversity, Mom walked by faith and not by sight.

Shawnee was gone, but Aubrey was not.

CHAPTER 6

There was one woman who could control and assuage Dad. This same woman was the confidante to my mom. That was one untouchable yet lovable person, his mother, my paternal grandmother Martha, more famously known as NaNa.

She was his numero uno. She was light and almost white in skin complexion. She was soft, and she was round. She was beautiful, and we loved her. Whatever she said was the final word and the end. Sure she spoiled him, but she also, understood, nurtured, and above all chastised him. Her favorite song was "Blessed Assurance." Dad would sing it in the pulpit on occasion before he would commence preaching. NaNa would just sit in the rear of the sanctuary and weep. Her baby boy was singing her favorite hymn to the glory of God. He knew the effect that song had on NaNa. He knew the effect it had on him.

Whenever Dad would mistreat my mom, all she had to do was make a call to NaNa and she would handle it.

Oh yeah, NaNa and Mom were best friends. The Zathers and the Carnegies finally became family. They talked every day. Mom learned secret family recipes from NaNa. My siblings' and Dad's favorite was cornbread dressing. Mom and NaNa would spend unfeigned quality time together. They knew each other's schedule. They would talk on the phone once Mom got us off to school. Then when NaNa's soap operas came on, they would retire until later in the day. Then NaNa would take a nap, wake, fix dinner, and eat. Then Mom and NaNa would talk on the phone again.

It was a phone relationship yet a powerful relationship. They would usually see one another weekly at church and on holidays. What I would soon find out was that they were one another's refuge in time of myriad storms.

NaNa treated Mom as one of her own daughters, so much that sometimes her own daughters would show envy toward my mother. They would constantly call attention to what they perceived as some of Mom's shortcomings. "Celeste needs to keep a cleaner house and take better care of her children." This notion would resound after Mom's return from the hospital after giving birth to her fourth child. Mom didn't have the help that she needed to maintain a clean house, cook dinner, satisfy Dad, and care for the kids.

Mom was twenty-four with four kids. She was a pastor's wife, and she was tired. But her sisters-in-law made her appear and feel unfit, unacceptable, and unworthy. The mockery didn't stop NaNa. She supported Mom until the end. Celeste was her favorite. PaPa, my paternal grandfather, was also fond of Mom. After NaNa's death, this would be as clear as O. J.'s guilt for crimes one, two, or three.

There was an undeniable familial transformation when NaNa became ill. She was diagnosed with having emphysema. She had smoked cigarettes pretty much all of her life, as would most of the Carnegie family, my dad included. Great uncles died from it, great aunts died from it, uncles died from it, and aunts died from it. Smoking cigarettes had become a deadly generational curse in the Carnegie family.

After all the funerals I began to wonder, "Don't they see the dangers of smoking those cancer sticks?" I hated the smell of cigarettes and vowed never to smoke them. At times, my Mom and my siblings would dread going to my grandparents' for holidays because the smoke-filled home would just be too unbearable.

NaNa finally stopped smoking in order to help alleviate some of the noticeable and detrimental effects. However, her cessation was too late. The cancer had ravished and was now tormenting her body. The physical debacle was a tragic sight to witness. The family would sit by daily and watch her impending demise; there was no other way to look at it. We would visit on a daily basis in hopes of soothing and supporting the one we had come to know as the glue that held the Carnegie family together.

It was NaNa who would always make sure we had festive holiday gatherings, come hell or high water. It was NaNa who would dilute that pain of hurt, whether it was from a playground fall or a family fall out. It was NaNa who would save the day. I loved her. We all loved her. We all lost her.

PaPa went crazy. The family separated, and part of Dad was irreparably damaged. When he came home after first receiving the news of NaNa's death, Dad held Caren and me tightly as he cried uncontrollably. His expression of grief was a sight I had never seen and would never witness again. It was both scary and emotional. Dad was now in his weakest state. He was so fragile.

"Oh, God no, not my mom," he would repeatedly lament. Only God would be able to quench the volcano that was slowly but inevitably erupting inside Dad. From that point on when Dad would sing "Blessed Assurance," he would be the one alone weeping without NaNa.

No sooner than we laid NaNa to rest then we admitted PaPa to the hospital. He was, as would be frequently called, "speeding." He wouldn't think, he would just move; he wouldn't rest, he would just go. My grandparents had been married for close to five decades, and the death of NaNa was heavier for him still. PaPa was in an unhealthy emotional and physical predicament. And Dad, the omniscient kid of the Carnegie clan, had to figure out what to do for his father, for his family, and still for his church.

PaPa was hospitalized. Yet, after much ordained prayer and legal medication, he was allowed to come home. His oldest daughter, Bonita, moved in with him in hopes of assisting him in the time of need. Her assistance would turn into annoyance, as far as we could see. She was soon evicted. PaPa rented her an apartment and sent her on her way. He was back and back with a vengeance.

While PaPa revisited his independence, Dad continued to mask his own improprieties by buying us pacification things. Gifts became his love language. They were things we all agreed meant nothing if Mom hurt, we hurt, and ultimately God's bride, the church, hurt. Amid the guilt gifts, late-night meetings, and consequential bad tempers, an unwarranted alienation persisted.

Mom became weak. Sure she was God's child. She loved God and wanted the best for herself and her children. She wanted us to have the father she never had. But she concluded that she could no longer endure the disrespect, debasement, and destruction that the relationship sustained. Mom told Dad she wanted a divorce. Where was NaNa when you needed her?

No one believed it—not us, not Mom's or Dad's family, not the church, and certainly not Dad. I knew that he was surprised and hurt, yet he maintained his dignity and granted her the wish. After all, now he would have the legal and acceptable privilege to carry on as he wished with whomever and however.

The announcement came on a soft and quiet spring day. We had all come home from school. It was a day that I will never forget. Dad called all the siblings to the kitchen: "Angel, Caren, Tonya, Preston II, Grover, Felicia, and Katie, come here. Your mom has something to tell you guys." In an angelic and cautionary way, Mom stated, "Your dad and I are getting a divorce."

The pronouncement pierced my heart like a knife. We were all in awe. "No way. Yeah, right. Why?" were the many sounds being echoed in the room. Dad responded, "This is what your mom wants." He continued, "I told her that we could get counseling, but she doesn't want it." Another burden to carry. Why do children perpetually get blamed for parent's moronic morass. Parents give birth to children, not the other way around. "Wake up, parents." Have a heart.

"*No!*" Mom emphatically charged. She was tired. "It should be finalized by the time you start college, Angel." The news was too unheard of, too unthinkable for us to truly respond. But we reacted as if it was a joke and Mom would eventually change her mind. But she never did.

This was the summer that I was to begin college. We packed my belongings and whisked me off to a new beginning from the end of where I had begun, Dad and Mom. Although the commute was only an hour long, the separation was in some ways eternal. I cried when Dad left my dorm room. Although I knew that the matriculation was a new positive start for me, it would be the end of the balance and symmetry of my family. Dad moved out. Mom stayed. I moved on.

CHAPTER 7

Upon entering my first semester at college, Dad decided to marry Aubrey. What nerve. The nuptials wounded the heart of both families, biological and spiritual. The ugly truth was finally unmasked, made public, and brought out of the darkness and into a nebulous haze. The symmetry had become unbalanced by an unforgivable, unwarranted, unintended sin. Here's how the events went down.

Although I was only an hour from home away at school, I was kept abreast of everything as if I were living in the same neighborhood. Aubrey started openly calling the house, boldly spending time with , and dating Dad. You name it, *she* was involved.

On the day of the wedding, which I did not attend, I received a call from my siblings. I told them to call me immediately after the rushed, weekday, clandestine ritual concluded.

The events went as follows. As Aubrey walked down the aisle, my sister Tonya ran out crying. Dad followed. He told her that everything would be all right. He had a way of telling people what they needed to hear in order to satisfy their immediate fears and his ultimate desire. The ceremony resumed. The service was completed. Dad married *she*.

Dad and Aubrey lived together in an apartment not two miles from the home that he previously shared with Mom and the kids. How sick. How selfish. The kids remained with Mom. Although the distance made it easy for the kids to visit with Dad, the company did not. They loved Dad but despised the visit.

With the adverse history preceding the union, it was hard for us to accept Dad's new addition. We remembered the stares at church, the late nights Dad kept, the tears Mom cried, and the division we witnessed. The nightmare all happened so fast and so undeservedly.

The kids would tell me, "You were right all along, Angel. Dad was cheating on Mom, and he does love Aubrey." But was it love or lust? We determined that it was not the kingdom love that we had been taught from the Holy Bible. And now the rumors that we had heard became more believable.

Maybe Dad had in fact slept with Debbie, Jackie, and Pam. Dad had become dishonest, unbelievable, and unacceptable. We loved him, but we abhorred his actions. We wanted to see him but hated the sight of him.

But since I was looked upon as the one who set the bad virus in motion because I told Mom, Dad asked me to be accepting of his selfish familial design and help the kids to understand what was going on. Imagine that. I hated the aberration the most. How could I help an ailing horse that I wished I could just shoot and take it out of its misery?

Being the caring, incomparable woman that Mom was, she implored me to let God handle it. She was always reciting Proverbs 3:5–6: "Trust in the Lord with all your heart and lean not on your own understanding; in all your ways acknowledge him, and he will make your paths straight."

I heard Mom's exhortation yet reasoned that I would help God along to deliver us from this farcical and treacherous situation. The task was going to be harder than I thought.

Once on a visit home from college, I needed, as most college kids, of course, to pick up some money from Dad. He told me to come to the house to get it. Was he serious? He wanted to rub my face right in the dung. Some of my siblings sprang up. "I want to go with you. We have got to see this."

They knew Aubrey would be there and wanted to see how I would react. I saw her in church earlier in the day but ignored her like habitual smokers do the label on a box of cigarettes. To me, she was cancerous. The feeling was something I couldn't deny. For years, I had studied her spirit, and it was something that I was never comfortable with.

Dad said he would gladly give me the money, so I could no longer disregard her. I was forced to encounter her.

My siblings and I walked into the apartment. There Aubrey was lying on the couch in a soft, silk robe with a head full of horse hair. She always wore hair weaves. Aubrey could never really grow hair. She only had a small afro. Since she wanted to be so much like my Mom, who had naturally grown beautiful, long, and healthy hair, she would purchase the entire donkey's tail in order to get the long hair effect. Now Aubrey's hair was as long as Samson's.

I walked in and gave Dad a hug. Dad said, "Did you speak to Aubrey?"

I looked, and in the most reluctant and reprehensible tone said, "Hi."

Just making that simple gesture hurt so badly. I thought here was the woman who had strategically, selfishly, and sinfully taken my father and my family and repositioned us into something that was once planted on a firm foundation but was now on quicksand.

I felt as if no one else could see the despair but me. I felt so all alone. I wanted to ask, "Hello, is there anybody else home? Does anyone see the damage that has taken place in my familial situation?"

Dad immediately tried to move on to other topics of discussion. "How's school? How's cheerleading? How are your friends?" All questions were answered with a one- or two-word reply. But the small talk didn't help. Everyone knew it.

After the indifferent quandary of questions, I got the money and we left. The heat was hot, not only in the kitchen, but also in the church. After the wedding, the church membership suffered. The decline had an adverse effect on the size of the Sunday morning offering. Scarcity would tempt Dad to complain about the court-ordered child support.

He would voice that contributing to his seed was hard for him, since he wasn't making what he used to make in the Sunday offerings. He had less money and couldn't pay for your kids. I didn't get it. This was all a consequence of sin. We wrestle not against flesh and blood but against powers and wickedness in high places. I reasoned that Aubrey was putting pressure on him.

This pressure that prompted Dad to do the things he did was beginning to bludgeon him to the point of bursting. He was back to snapping and being stressed, and most of all the selfishness he exuded intensified. Aubrey was now getting a taste of what my mom had experienced from Dad for most of her life.

The Discipleship congregation still loved Mom and the once-beloved union, no matter how nonsymmetrical it had become. They felt betrayed because they were taught by Dad that God could handle anything, including the loss of a job, a drug-addicted family member, a sick child, death, and sin. But what had happened here? What is the approach for divorce? Does God's perspective change?

The chain of events was like a domino effect. Within the church community, there was one divorce after another. After my parents' divorce, within the year, five other couples in the congregation would divorce. These were couples who had been married for over fifteen years.

An ex-husband from one of the divorced couples would in future intimate to me that his wife said, "If Reverend and Celeste can get a divorce, then it is okay for us to get one." Our family devastation brought on other depressing situations. The paradigm shift was like a plague had just ripped through the temple. The church had always respected Dad and Mom. But now, because of their selfish act, people were confused, resentful, and sinful. Righteousness exalts a nation, but sin is a reproach.

I can recall a high school friend once explained to me how he was hurt after learning about what happened to my family and the church. He said, "Your dad's spirited, youthful style of preaching the gospel is what led me and my friends to Jesus. We used to love going to church. You guys always had the best-looking family, and I looked up to your dad. But now we question what was the preaching really about? Can I trust ministers?"

That statement would resonate in my life for perpetuity. Subsequently my friend's entire family, mom, sister, and friends would eventually leave the church. Nonetheless, I had to continue on, go back to school, and be strong from a distance for the family and for the future.

Meanwhile, Shawnee moved back to Cambridge. This time she chose to live in a house that her maternal grandmother owned. She was now older and different, we thought. We saw her occasionally. Things were somewhat changed.

She was pregnant. Initially it was a shock. Dad was mad. He knew that her choice of men was not good. Yet intuitively we knew a pregnancy was bound to happen. She had grown up in the fast life of Colorado. She was pregnant by a notorious bad guy who was a thug and also a small-time Cambridge drug dealer.

Shawnee was attracted to that lifestyle. It was a lifestyle that she and her child would have to deal with at least for the next eighteen years. But we all, momentarily, got over the thoughts of consternation. We were excited about our first niece or nephew being born.

Dina, a beautiful baby girl, was born. Everyone was elated. We bragged. We boasted. She was cute. She was a Carnegie; she was part of the clan. She would be the piece that would coagulate the bond in the Carnegie clan. It was inexplicable, but it was like we loved Dina more than Shawnee. It was an ironic yet surprisingly understandable situation. We thought Dina's birth would be something that would bring the siblings closer together.

There was still something about Shawnee. That feeling of separation and differentials could not be denied—different moms, different upbringings, different spirits. Nonetheless, the relationship healed a bit, but ultimately the past would be revisited and we would always know that our sisterhood would be in question.

Blood is not always thicker than water. Satan would make sure to always remind us.

Aubrey "loved" our new niece. She was a babysitter and a substitute grandmother. She bought her lots of clothes and toys. Shawnee was happy, despite what she knew about Aubrey. Getting money and things instead of love was the only kind of relationship she was used to. Shawnee was raised to believe that if someone bought you something, you had better reciprocate the kindness.

Since she was allegedly abused as a child by her mother and boyfriends, she would take kindness where she could get it, and for any price. Although Shawnee always liked my mom, she was motivated to gravitate to the gifts and money given to her by Aubrey.

That's how the situation affected Shawnee. The motivation didn't matter because she never developed the love that our family shared. Our kind of love denounced the notion of someone trying to invade, corrupt, or annihilate.

Shawnee was blood but not complete blood. She was our half-sister. At times we almost thought that she was befriending Aubrey on purpose just to make us mad. Arguably she probably was, but it was of no consequence to us. We didn't like Aubrey, anyway. The Bible speaks of consequences of blended families in Genesis 21:9-13 and Galatians chapter 4. Heed the call families of God.

Dad and Aubrey moved into a ranch-style home in a low- to middle-class neighborhood. It was a long way from the five-bedroom home he once shared with Mom and the kids. We would eventually find out that Aubrey's parents helped her get the home. While Dad tried to start a new home and family, his other family started to feel the wrath of the ole evil one, the deluder, Satan.

Although Dad paid court-ordered child support, it was not enough. I was in college, and my siblings were ever growing. Mom's house was in constant need of upkeep and maintenance. Mom worked two jobs day and night in order to supplement the meager child support. All the while, Caren, now a sophomore in high school, was staying out doing what she thought was acceptable. She was partying, carousing, and keeping company with the people that Dad had trained us to believe were unacceptable.

I was home for summer break, and I could not believe my eyes. Caren had become friends with an infamous drug dealer. I knew him from high school. He was once a good churchgoing kid who had now turned to the streets.

It was summer time. The temperature was hot, along with the emotions in and around my home. Mom alerted Dad of Caren's carousing. Once he found out, the volcano blew its top.

Dad came over and reprimanded, scolded, and degraded Caren in a way I had never witnessed before. Caren and her new friend were returning from a date. Dad ran to the car yelling and chastising Caren, "You are a tramp. You better start respecting yourself and your mother." He continued yelling, but now to the guy, "I better not ever see you around my house again." I reflected, "His house. What a thought." That was a joke.

Caren, in shock, thought that was the funniest thing. After all, what was respect in a home of a man who committed adultery and left the family who always looked to him for provision, protection, and power? Caren was undeniably hurt. I believe it took a long time for her to get over that experience. In future we would understand why when she finally went away to college, she rarely returned home for visits.

That night's events and Dad's tirade did not impede Caren's progress. She continued to remain good in sports and maintained her academic honor roll status. Unfortunately, she would continue to hang out with and have sex with some unspeakable types of people. But by the grace, she excelled in her life. Proverbs 19:21 reads…Many are the plans of a man's heart, but God's purpose prevails.

CHAPTER 8

The first Christmas after Mom's divorce from Dad and his subsequent marriage to Aubrey was bad. On previous Christmas Eves we would go to NaNa and PaPa's house and exchange gifts. Albeit filled with cigarette smoke and attitudes from my aunts to Mom, it was the holiday and it was family. The Carnegie family, Dad, Mom, sisters, brothers, cousins, and friends would gather together sing Christmas carols, light the fireplace, bake cookies, and anxiously await Christmas. We had the best time. We adored it. But it all changed. NaNa was gone. Mom and Dad were done.

Now we saw Dad briefly on Christmas Eve. And on Christmas, he came over and gave us the gifts from Mom and Dad. He ate a little something (who could resist NaNa's recipe for cornbread dressing?), and then he left. We were then required to go over to his home and receive gifts that Aubrey and her parents had purchased for us. We were lucky to have so many Christmas gifts. There was just one thing; we did not want them. We only went because of the selfish and earnest request from Dad and the motherly encouragement from Mom.

We went with anger in our hearts, even on Christmas. The emotions were hard to explain. We all sensed an unrest, a spirit that did not exhibit peace. Since God is not the author of confusion, the spirit had to have been designed by Satan.

Anytime we were around Aubrey, whether with her family or not, there was the uneasy, unwelcome spirit. Proverbs 5:3–6 reads: "For the lips of an adulteress drip honey, and her speech is smoother than oil; but in the end she is bitter as gall, sharp as a double-edged sword. Her feet go down to death; her steps lead straight to the grave. She gives no thought to the way of life; her paths are crooked, but she knows it not."

The new Dad-ordained Carnegie home was a tension-filled room, house, atmosphere, and world. The siblings' main objective was to get in and get out. With coats on, we opened the gifts, gave melancholy thanks, and left. We Carnegie children were incensed. We were sad. We were alone. Dad knew it, and he knew something had to be done.

As the New Year progressed, Dad started to come around more often. Some would say the reunion was because he cared. Others surmised the truth; it was because Mom was keeping new male company. One associate was Dad's father and the other a male friend of the Carnegie family.

When PaPa lost NaNa, he also lost his mind. He soon recovered, but he was different. He was "speeding" again. With the new pace, he found a penchant for dating younger women. Ironically, he chose his daughter in-law.

Mom perceived the time spent as developing a closer relationship with her father-in-law. Dad saw it as a dirty old man trying to take his ex-wife. PaPa would spend time at the house. He and Mom would go to dinner, plays, and movies. Dad warned Mom. Mom rejected his warnings. She thought the accusations were repulsive. PaPa had been her father-in-law for over twenty years.

She would intimate to Caren and me that Dad was unnecessarily jealous, and "If he keeps up, he's going to drive himself crazy." Everyone was vying for Mom's affections: Dad, PaPa, and the family friend. As far as we kids could tell, PaPa was winning. He was even winning us over. He would take us shopping and give us money. He even enrolled Tonya into piano lessons.

Papa invited Mom to a concert in Cleves. She was excited. Dad was infuriated. His siblings were aghast. She went, and Dad took notes. It was a trip that Mom would never forget. PaPa made a sexual pass at Mom. When he kissed her on the lips, he tried to put his tongue in her mouth. She was disgusted.

Mom hinted to Dad what had happened, and from that moment on Mom's objective was to eliminate and sever ties with PaPa. But PaPa was relentless. He was our grandpa, so he continued to come around. He said that he was checking on his grandchildren. He was another one who was used to getting his way. Although PaPa would continue to come around the house, he would for some reason slowly begin to reject Mom.

PaPa would start to have myriad of other younger women. The ladies knew that he had a bottomless bank account, and they all wanted some of it. He had so many women at the church as his associates that it had become a nuisance. Some women would hate to see him coming and would make a report, a clarion call to Dad, "Do something about your father. He is a pervert." Dad would demand PaPa to stop.

The demand would breed threats from Papa to Dad. It was a scary situation. He even came by the church on a Sunday morning and threatened Dad with a gun. Dad was emotionally hurt and embarrassed, yet incensed. He would downplay the encounter. What could he really do? PaPa was his father. The tides would subside when resisted. Resist the devil and he will flee. But this one would come back for another victim—a younger, unsuspecting victim; an innocent family member.

CHAPTER 9

Tonya loved PaPa. She had begun to spend quantity time with him. She would compel Mom to take her over to his home after school, or she would walk to PaPa's house. She just had to see her PaPa.

He would teach her, and at times along with a teacher, how to play piano. He would also teach her how to cook. He would eventually teach her something that would impact and affect her life for time without end. He bought her clothes, perfume, and candy and gave her money. It was the kind of granddaughter-grandpa relationship that some would perceive as uncommon and inappropriate. The relationship was like he was courting her. He would call her on the phone and pick her up to go to his house for visits. Even the siblings started to feel that PaPa loved Tonya more than the rest of us.

Mom was concerned. She remembered what had happened to her by the hands and lips of PaPa. One day Mom just snapped. She went over to Papa's and demanded that he let Tonya go. Behind the locked doors and windows, Papa told my Mom to go away. Mom banged and banged, but to no avail. Mom decided to call Dad. He was able to come over and convince PaPa to let Tonya go. She appeared physically unharmed, and they went home. Tonya was not allowed to return to PaPa's house.

Soon after the encounter, Tonya called me at college. She said, "Angel, PaPa did something to me."

"What?" I asked with fear and consternation in my voice.

"He molested me."

"Like how?" I couldn't understand, nor did I want to imagine what had happened to my sister at the hands of our grandpa.

She continued, "He would buy me lots of things and then told me not to tell. It was nasty. He would put my tits in his mouth and lick them. I couldn't move. I would let him do it. And he would touch me on my vagina."

I was speechless for a moment. Then I said, "I'm telling Dad."

She said, "Okay."

I called Dad immediately and told him to come and get me from college. He inquired, "What's up?"

I replied, "I have something very important to tell you that I can not relate to you over the phone."

Tonya had chosen to tell me and only me. And now I, the oldest, had to tell our Dad that his father molested his daughter. On the way home, all I remember hearing was Mom's precious voice reciting, "In all thy ways acknowledge Him and he will direct your path." I knew God would lead me and give me the words to say.

The drive home was a pathless maze. I didn't know where to start or how to end. My grandpa was a sick pervert and I had to be the one to tell Dad. Again, I had to be the one to spread the news about a bad virus.

I sat Mom and Dad down and blurted out, "PaPa has been molesting Tonya."

Instantly, a feeling of disbelief, guilt, and shame began to permeate the room. They both at once blurted, "When? How long? What do you mean?" There was utter confusion. I told them not to be mad at Tonya, "She already feels like crap." She didn't want to tell, but she was beginning to get more fearful of PaPa.

Dad was pissed. Mom was sad. The siblings who understood were disgusted. Dad was on his way to either confront Papa or kill him. Either way, Mom stopped him. She convinced him to let the courts handle it. But to this day, I believe the choice not to take some kind of immediate action against his dad still haunts my dad. I believe mom feels guilty too.

The inquiry opened up a mysterious box of mayhem that would surprise even Pandora's Box.

As time and further inquiry would reveal, PaPa had molested one of our cousins, his grandchild, and was presently molesting one of the children of his girlfriend. Our late grandma, NaNa, knew of PaPa's sickness. Dad's siblings knew it. They chose to keep it quiet. Dad didn't know what to do.

Because PaPa had been diagnosed as bipolar and was now on lithium, the judge said he would do no time. We reasoned that PaPa had the money to get out of serving prison time. He had been a thrifty truck driver for almost fifty years, was living off investments and retirement, and was still working as a limo driver for the local airport. He had money. PaPa didn't see a day in jail. He was ordered into a facility for observation.

The resolve was disheartening. Tonya became more alienated and alone. She was the only one not breastfed, and now she was also the only one of us siblings who had been molested by PaPa. The titles became too much for her to handle. She was in search of love—love from someone, somehow.

Meanwhile, Dad became angry, more ashamed, and more hostile. And amid the despair in our home and the desolate pews in the church, Dad knew he had to do something logical and sacrificial. Dad could be sagacious yet reasonable when it counted. He divorced Aubrey and began to court Mom again.

Now here I am a senior in college, and I thought what they were trying to teach me at times was confusing. Boy, the circumstances of my life could give my professors an impassable course in life.

Mom had lost weight. She felt young and beautiful again. It was as if she was atop the hill and displaying her hula hoop skills again. She welcomed the smooth, charismatic wooing of her first and only earthly love, Dad. They had begun dating again. They went to the movies, out to dinner, out for ice cream, you name it. If it had anything to do with sharing, they did it. The courtship appeared beautiful, innocent, and spiritual. But we kids remained skeptical.

What did Dad do with Aubrey? What were his intentions? Where do we the family and the church go from here? Mom's family told her that she was crazy. "Celeste, Preston hasn't changed. He's just up to something, nothing good. If you want to bump your head again, go ahead."

Mom was similar to and stubborn like my maternal grandma. She too did what she wanted. She wanted her family together. On the surface, our family was the complete family that she never had the opportunity to experience as a child. Our family had the father that she wanted her children to have, no matter the cost.

PaPa died. The last years of his life were uneventful. In his will he requested to have a private ceremony with no pomp and no circumstance. The ceremony was just a viewing of the body. We viewed it, and we left. The burial was conducted by the in-house grave attendant. To this day, we rarely hear anyone reference him, his life, or his impact.

Mom and Dad continued to date. As I walked across the stage to receive my bachelor of arts degree, I walked into the hugs of Mom and Dad, together again. When I matriculated to college, they were divorcing. When I graduated college, they were reconciling.

CHAPTER 10

Next-level thinking is the reason I decided to continue my education. I was on the path to attain my master of arts degree directly after I received my BA. I was not mentally and emotionally prepared to completely enter the workforce, yet I was very prepared to continue learning. I decided to attend the college where my sister Caren was a junior. We decided to live together in an apartment off campus.

Not only had I started next-level thinking, but I had an experience with a new beau. I began exclusively dating one of the most skilled and professional athletes in American history. The details of this and other relationships will be discussed in a forthcoming communication.

This relationship would change not only my life but also my dad, who would partner with the celebrity as a business associate and procure financial livelihood for family members and other persons in the community for years to come.

Our phone rang. It was Mom and Dad. They had decided to remarry. This decision came six months after their courtship, a year after Dad's divorce from Aubrey, and four years after my parents' first marriage of eighteen years ended. What was going on?

Caren and I couldn't believe it. When Dad told us about the pending nuptials, we couldn't respond. "We thought this was what you kids wanted," replied Dad.

"Are you guys sure?" we quipped. Caren and I went as far as to arrogantly say, "We are out of the city, in college, and doing our own thing. Do what you both want." Again, parents should be aware of consequences that divorce and sin have on the family. We must continue to pray for God's grace and mercy so His royalty does truly reign in our lives.

We were speaking from hurt and confusion. We did not realize that their dating had matured to the level of remarriage. Parents should recognize that children can only take so much. Unsurprisingly, Mom and Dad remarried, but it only lasted for six months. They divorced again. Now who were the crazy and confused ones?

Dad was still cheating with Aubrey. He was mean to Mom, and wanting his way. Mom was still quiet, docile, and seeking God. But this debasement was the last straw. She decided to move as far away from Dad as she could. She went back to her roots in the state of Georgia.

Once again the family was separated, but they had never been separated by such great physical and emotional distance. Dad moved back into the house once habited by our family. Mom moved to Georgia. With her she took my brother and sister Grover and Katie.

Everything was out of sync. Caren and I were learning and partying in college. At times, it was a challenge for Caren to balance the two, with the latter winning the battle. I was studying hard, but every weekend I was flying out of town to California, Denver, and Illinois to spend time with my boyfriend.

Shawnee was back in Colorado with her daughter. Tonya, Preston II, and Felicia were in high school. They decided to stay with Dad. Grover and Katie were in Georgia with Mom. Finally, Dad was doing his thing. He was still being a pastor who spent all his time away at the church and most of that time being with Aubrey.

Meanwhile, Dad's teenage children were in the house raising themselves, drinking, not studying, hanging out, and being involved in other immoral teenage behavior.

Caren and I dreaded going home for visits. The environment was boring, tragic, and unwelcoming. Everyone was scattered somewhere. Some of the siblings were in the North and some in the South. There was no support system, no foundation, and no love. We were all looking for that which we were used to getting from our nucleus and immediate family, Dad, Mom, and siblings. Although our present familial representation was not the epitome of family strength, our family was built on the foundation of God.

I can recall us as a family, Dad, Mom, and seven siblings, gathering together in the living room for nightly prayer. We would gather hands, and from youngest to the oldest, each person would recite a prayer to God. My parents always recited, as did most Christian families at the time, "A family that prays together stays together."

Royalty Reigns In the grand scheme of things, and God's design for family is what we longed for. According to the Bible, the family is an impressive, majestic, and distinguished plan, representation, and idea of love between family members that is ordained by God and should be experienced and shared by Dad, Mom, and children.

We were taught from birth the Word of God. The Good Book represented from Genesis to Revelation the trials yet triumph of God's family. We wanted that love. We strove for that love.

John 3:16 reads, "For God so loved the world that he gave his only begotten son that whosoever believeth in him shall not perish, but have everlasting life." God is love, and his design is supposed to work. Under the circumstances we were having a hard time believing that his proposal was going to work in our family and in our future.

Mom was feeling desertion and pain as a result of making the decision to move to Georgia. She thought a move was a cure-all; out of sight, out of mind. But the younger siblings were not doing well in school in the South. They were always physically sick. The older siblings in the North were getting in where they fit in with mediocre grades and friends who used them.

We were all putting up a façade of joy yet plastered by a wall of pain.

My graduation was nearing. I attained my MA in a year's time. Tonya was soon to be graduating high school. I dumped my professional athlete boyfriend and moved decided to move to the south the mom after graduation. Tonya matriculated into the college I attended for my MA She was now at school with Caren. Our life was on a fast track again, when we should have done as God says in Psalm 46 verse 10, "Be still and know that I am God."

It took six months of convincing, but Mom, Grover, Katie, and I moved back to Cambridge. Hallelujah.

CHAPTER 11

We pulled up in the U-haul truck and Mom's car. The reunion was bittersweet. The family was semi-together yet not together. "Praise God, we made it," we recited as we walked through the front door of the house. Dad quickly ran to the door and said to Mom, "What are you doing here?"

Mom, in a reserved and defeated tone, replied, "You said that you wanted us to come back home."

"Yeah, but I thought that you were going to stay with your sister Jocelyn."

In previous weeks, Dad had continually implored Mom to come back to Cambridge. We later found out his motives were selfish, political, and child-support related. He couldn't handle the responsibility of the kids, the church, and his woman.

Dad began physically pushing Mom and saying, "You are not coming back in here. Don't even bring your stuff in this house." She was shocked and hurt. I was hurt, the siblings were confused. My cousin

Jerry, who helped us move back to Cambridge, jumped in the middle and said to Dad, "Hold it, you are not going to disrespect my aunt." Dad backed off.

We loaded ourselves back into the U-haul truck and car and traveled to Aunt Jocelyn's house. "Dad is mean. I can't stand him," was the echo of my siblings. We told the story to Auntie Jocelyn. She could and couldn't believe it. "A tiger never changes its stripes," was her reply. But he was supposed to be a man of God, wasn't he?

Even though Mom was hurt, rejected, and alone, she knew what she had to do. She got a temporary job the next day. While we were unpacking and determining the next step, Dad called Mom with speedy and strange information. "Celeste, you can move into the house with the kids. I have found an apartment." The behavior sounded of one who needed medication. My grandpa was on lithium before he died. Based on Dad's discombobulated actions, I pray that he does not experience similar circumstances.

Before we could empty out the U-haul, we were moving back into the house once shared by my family—Dad, Mom, and kids. I am sure stranger things have happened, but I have yet to be made aware of them.

Caren was soon to graduate college with her bachelor of arts degree. Tonya was now on campus too. The other siblings were at the house. I decided to stay in Cambridge until I determined my next move. Dad was in his apartment alone—or so we thought. We were beginning to hear rumors that Dad and Aubrey were dating again. Are you serious?

"He must be crazy. She is ugly, bald (now she had started to wear a short afro instead of the long weaves), and she destroyed our family," was the unanimous response from the siblings. Aubrey had been completely bald for quite some time. She said that she had a disorder and had decided to go bald due to her feelings of liberation and boldness.

Isaiah 3:16–17 reads, "The Lord says, The women of Zion are haughty, walking along with outstretched necks, flirting with their eyes, tripping along with mincing steps, with ornaments jingling on their ankles. Therefore the Lord will bring sores on the heads of the women of Zion; the Lord will make their scalps bald."

I realize there are persons who legitimately have cancer and do go through chemotherapy, yet the timeliness and boldness of Aubrey's decision to go bald left many questions unanswered and inexplicable.

Preston II was becoming so dejected that he began to turn to liquor for solace. One night he got so drunk that he came home in a rage about Aubrey and dad's relationship. "I'm going to kill that bitch! She destroyed my family. I hate her." Not only was the liquor speaking but the many years of rejection, hurt, and confusion.

These were some of the many unkind blusters that Preston related to us amid the smell and influence of liquor. We said, "Did you tell Dad how you feel?" Of course he had not. From that revelation, we decided to jump into the car (with a sober sibling driving) and headed over to Dad's apartment.

We knocked on the door. Dad hesitantly said, "Who is it?"

"Your kids," was our reply.

"Wait a minute," was his reply. After about three minutes, he opened the door. We presumed his welcome took so long because Aubrey must have been hiding somewhere in the house.

"Hey, what do you guys want?" chuckled Dad.

In unison and with almost unrecognizable utterances, we grumbled, "Do you know what you are doing? Preston II is drunk and hurt, and Caren is alienated and emotional and physically abusing herself. Mom is hurt. Your family is broken. You have rejected us, all because of some sexual, spiritual, immoral desire.

"What is going on? How can you do this to us? You preach about family, and you let one woman destroy ours. Aubrey can't be that valuable." Dad was silent. We continued the banter. "What are you going to do?"

He finally spoke. "I didn't know that you all felt like this. Go home and I will come home tomorrow. You all are important to me." Good ole dad, always knowing how to diffuse a lively inferno. We hugged each other. Preston II sobbed uncontrollably. Dad held on to him tightly. We left. Victory was ours.

Dad came home but only for three months. The demonic pull of the Jezebel spirit, which is manipulative, oppressive, selfish, and prideful (refer to 1 Kings 21) was working in and through Aubrey. The pervasively selfish personality of Dad wouldn't let him honor his word. He was gone again. This time he decided to remarry Aubrey and made it quite clear that he didn't care what we, church members, friends, or anybody thought.

I want to make sure you, my readers, get the story straight. Dad and Mom married for eighteen years and then divorced. Dad married Aubrey (after the adulterous relationship with her) for two years and then divorced her. Then Dad remarried Mom for six months and then divorced her. Then Dad remarried Aubrey. But this time Aubrey refused to let go.

Slowly the church began to lose members. Dad began to lose the connection with those faithful fighting giant preachers that he once emulated and loved. Sutherland and Pruitt restricted visits to once a year or not at all. Dad was losing credibility in all his circles. But worst of all, Dad was losing his family.

Preston II decided to move as far away as possible. He joined the Air Force. Caren graduated from college and moved to south Indiana; I joined her. Tonya became pregnant and dropped out of college. She would eventually have three children. (The first two children have the same dad, the last a different one.)

The younger siblings were not doing well in school and were not physically healthy. (Katie developed viral meningitis but was eventually healthy.) Grover and Felicia were literally just existing, going to school, and hanging out. Shawnee and her daughter moved back to Cambridge.

But the greatest of these, Mom, was working two jobs, was lonely, and now was starting to drink. We couldn't believe it. The saint that we perceived her to be was now being deceived by Satan. She would ask my cousin Jerry to go and purchase for her a bottle of wine. He would sit around to watch her and make sure things didn't get out of hand. Mom had never been a drinker. Jerry, as well as everyone else, was concerned. The concern lasted only for a couple of nights. Psalm 30:5b reads, "Weeping may endure for a night, but joy cometh in the morning."

Praise God Mom's drinking only lasted for a week; it seemed like a year. It was strange timing, but thank God the redemption was true and immediate. Mom immediately got back to the Word of God and renewed her mind. She soon became an ordained minister.

Mom was now preaching deliverance to the captives. She was on fire for God. She soon joined a different church and moved into a home on the other side of town. Although the neighborhood was low-income and crime pervaded the territory, Mom was proud to say that the home was hers—something that she purchased on her own. She vowed that Dad would never have control over her again.

By this time, Mom was working in a factory, making favorable money. Mom was her own boss socially and monetarily. She was liberated. At times, she would continue to express her pain and sorrow because of the decimation of the family. Yet, her heart for Jesus wouldn't let her remain in pain. She would begin to take preaching engagements around the city while also serving as an associate minister at her new church home.

Tonya along with her children, and a female friend, as a paying roommate, and her daughter moved into our old family house. Dad allowed Tonya to live rent free. What was his motive?

Was it because he was trying to help or was it because he was trying to gain a friend in at least one child when the others had deserted him? Tonya had always been for the underdog so it was easy to win her over. Or was the gesture because of the historical and infamous fact that she wasn't breastfed? Or was it because she was alienated and rejected because of not only the emotional abuse experienced within the family, but the physical and sexual abuse inflicted on her by our grandfather? Nevertheless, Tonya continued to work, care for her kids, and attend Dad's church.

At this point, Dad had relocated his church to another location in the city. Dad and his congregation, by faith, purchased a large church complex from a nondenominational congregation in the community. The complex is situated on the north side of the city with a sanctuary, youth center, day-care center, and reception hall.

This was a major move for dad and Discipleship Missionary Baptist Church family, which was now named Discipleship Christian Church.

Dad decided to remove the Baptist title and connotation and replace it with the Christian Church in order to fulfill what he reasoned was the mandate of the Bible, not of the denomination. Since he founded the church, he had the power to make the change, with no questions asked of anyone. Some left the church, but by this time we didn't know if their departures were related to Dad's familial failures or the denominational directive. All the while, there was also a magnanimous shift ever present in life of Dad's immediate family.

Chapter 12

_____

Another collegiate legacy was at work in our family. Felicia graduated from the same college as Caren and I did. Grover joined the Air Force (stationed in Texas) like his older brother Preston II (now stationed in Nevada). Baby girl Katie was in high school. Although out of sight, we were all on one another's mind. I would visit them in Texas, Nevada, and Cambridge.

In my encounters I noticed that my brothers were abusing alcohol and had picked up the terrible and generational curse of smoking cigarettes. At the home front, the girls just seemed to be dejected and not the naturally beautiful, radiant young ladies they had once been. I was overly consumed with my life, my studies, and my objectives, whatever they were at the time. Caren was kicking it hard. Tonya was drinking and unstable, although she always managed to keep a job. She knew that she had to take care of her kids. Shawnee was working and trying to find her place within all the family crises. By this time, her birth mother had moved to Cambridge and was now on drugs.

Dad and Aubrey were pretending that everything was blissful, but I would constantly hear word from my siblings that, "Dad snaps at and curses her just like he used to do to Mom." Actually, Dad and Aubrey were just bearing one another. They each had a hidden agenda. It had been self-orchestrated, and via evil demons, spiritually manifested. But ultimately the mission would backfire. Contrary to popular belief, the grass is not always greener on the other side. It is true.

Dad was drinking, and not just water. He had begun drinking strong drink. Aubrey cosigned the indulgence. They were involved in dissipation. On the surface, they were doing the will of God on Sunday. But on Monday through Saturday, their lives were a free for all: smoking, drinking, and living in misery. The Kingdom of God is love, peace, and righteousness. An obvious dichotomy, a war between flesh and spirit, was at work in Dad's life.

I never witnessed the behavior firsthand, but again my siblings kept me fully abreast of the situation. I couldn't believe it. Yet, as I continued to grow in my faith in Jesus and the Word of God, situations like these started to make more sense. In Jude verse 18 it reads, "These are murmurers, complainers, walking after their own lusts; and their mouth speaketh great swelling words, having men's persons in admiration because of advantage. But, beloved remember ye the words which were spoken before the apostles of our Lord Jesus Christ; How that they told you there should be mockers in the last time, who should walk after their own ungodly lusts." Dad was in a war, and mom's battle was not far behind.

I don't know if it was loneliness or rebellion, but Mom decided to begin dating again. This mandate came after she made a decree to never date or be involved with a man ever again. She would say, "Jesus is my boyfriend."

Although Mom kept Jesus, she also took up with someone else. Tom was his name. Trickery and manipulation were his game. How he wormed his way into Mom's life only the deception revealed in the third chapter in the book of Genesis could explain.

He was an ex-con, an ex-drug addict, an ex-husband, an ex-you name it. If it was unsavory, Tom had done it. He had somehow convinced Mom that he had changed his life around from good to bad and was now seeking to live for Jesus.

Coincidentally, Tom had begun attending Mom's church. Ironically, over forty years before, Mom had dated Tom. Although the encounter was brief, a past spark had been reignited. Tom persuaded Mom that he was her knight in shining armor. The courtship started with them watching movies together, cooking together, and going to church together. A month later, they were married. Are you serious?

To this day I have still never met this man. Yet, according to the reports of my siblings, aunts, uncles, and Dad, Tom was never right for Mom. Although we wanted her to find genuine love, happiness, and family, Tom was not the one.

Within a month after the private ceremony, which was not attended by family, Tom began stealing from Mom. He was a crack addict. Drug addicts have to have their drug fix. He didn't have a job, so the only way he could get what he desired was to ask Mom or steal from Mom. Tom, more often, chose the latter.

Mom had a garage full of valuables. These things included DVDs, TVs, tire rims, computers, and furniture. These valuables belonged to my siblings. One day Felicia wanted to retrieve something of hers from the garage. She opened the door and there was nothing. Mom's garage had been completely cleaned out.

According to my siblings' calculations, close to ten thousand dollars worth of stuff was gone. There were no more TVs, DVDs, nothing.

We all knew who did it. Mom reported it to the police, but they never resolved or made an arrest.

We begged Mom to divorce Tom. She reminded us that she was watching and praying. She told us, "I know something is going on, and I will deal with it soon." From that moment on, we all knew that it was war time.

Ephesians 6:10–13 reads, "Finally, be strong in the Lord and in his might power. Put on the full armor of God so that you can take your stand against the devil's schemes. For our struggle is not against flesh and blood, but against the rulers, against the authorities, against the powers of this dark world and against the spiritual forces of evil in the heavenly realms. Therefore put on the full armor of God, so that when the day of evil comes, you may be able to stand your ground, and after you have done everything, to stand."

The family, aunties, uncles, and siblings banded together to intercede and pray for mom. Thirty years before, Mom and the siblings prayed for the devil to be rebuked from Dad's life, and now we were praying the evil one to be rebuked from Mom's life. What a turnaround.

Although Caren and I lived in south Indiana, at prayer time, we touched and agreed via the telephone. Matthew 18:19–20 reads, "Again, I tell you that if two of you on earth agree about anything you ask for, it will be done for you by my Father in heaven. For where two or three come together in my name, there am I with them."

We prayed that God would take the blinders off Mom's eyes and release her from this stronghold of shame and evil. My aunties were crying, and my sisters were weeping. We were beseeching God to do a mighty and immediate work of redemption for my Mom. The scenario of evil was so confusing. But God is all powerful. With God all things are possible.

The one who appeared to be rooted and grounded in the Word of God was now being deceived and tricked by an evil, ugly, and oppressive spirit being used in the body of Tom. But God is faithful, and we had to remember and believe that. First Timothy 3:3 reads, "But the Lord is faithful, and he will strengthen and protect you from the evil one."

CHAPTER 13

Dad needed heart surgery. The doctors found an abnormality in one of his heart valves. An immediate and necessary surgery was eminent. This was much to our alarm, because Dad had never been really ill. He had lymph nodes removed in outpatient surgery but never anything of this magnitude.

Dad would be out of commission for at least three months and had physical therapy for the next year. It was a life altering and prayerful season for the Carnegie clan. Now we were praying for Mom's redemption and Dad's complete healing and recovery.

During this time in my life, I rehearsed and read Second Timothy 3:1–7. It reads, "But mark this: There will be terrible times in the last days. People will be lovers of themselves, lovers of money, boastful, proud, abusive, disobedient to their parents, ungrateful, unholy, without love, unforgiving, slanderous, without self-control, brutal, not lovers of the good, treacherous, rash, conceited, lovers of pleasure rather than lovers of God—having a form of godliness but denying its power. Have nothing to do with them. They are the kind who worm their way into homes and gain control over weak-willed women who are loaded down with sins and are swayed by all kinds of evil desires, always learning but never able to acknowledge the truth."

Supernaturally, this principle helped me to understand many familial situations from a personal perspective and as it relates to my siblings.

Here's the family rundown. Dad, who was preparing for heart surgery (from which he is presently making recovery) was married to manipulative, sinister spirit of Aubrey for the second time. Then there was Mom, who was constantly running to the hospital with her sick, drug-addicted, and treacherous husband, Tom.

I was now married to a nightclub owner. A preacher's kid and a nightclub owner—who would have thought such a diametrically opposed kind of marital union could be possible? A year later in this union we had twin boys. I was also studying to receive my PhD in educational leadership and administration.

Caren was married with two kids and studying to receive her MA in educational leadership. For some reason, she always wanted to be like her big sister. Mom tells the story best. "Angel when you joined the choir, Caren wanted to join. When you went somewhere, Caren wanted to go." The sibling connection continues unto this day. Caren and I were still living in southern Indiana.

Tonya was now on her own and living with her three children. Dad had since decided to sell our home, and Tonya was living elsewhere. Preston II received an administrative dismissal from the military, was living back in Cambridge, and was divorced twice. With the first marriage came the birth of his two daughters. Felicia was a recent college graduate, living back in Cambridge. Grover was now medically discharged from the military, married with three kids, and living back in Cambridge. Katie, now a college dropout, was living in Cambridge with her twin girls. Shawnee was living in Cambridge with her three children.

What a brief familial synopsis of what was once defined by the Cambridge League as the "Family of the Year." More than that, this was the family who rehearsed and lived, "A family that prays together, stays together." Where had we gone wrong?

I recall an email sent to me from Dad before I got married. It should shed some light on the unsavory, unhealthy, and unhappy situation that the Carnegie clan now finds it. It reads in part:

> I have been trying to write you for some time now. I am very concerned and hurt by the way you are handling our relationship. For quite a long time you have chosen to distance yourself from me because you chose not to accept the fact that your mother and I are divorced and that I am now married to Aubrey. Your mother and I had some good times and unfortunately many bad times. We both tried to do the best for our children and give all of you the best of our love, provision, and guidance. We both made some mistakes and we both played a part in the dismantling of our marriage, whether you believe it or not. But you have chosen to try to hold me hostage because I have gone on with my life. I am sorry that your mother and I didn't work things out, but those are the facts. I am also sorry that your dream world doesn't line up with the real world. Angel, all of us have been hurt deeply. Any family that goes through what we have experiences deep pain. But if there is any real love, it overrides the anger, hurt, and disappointment and rallies to love that remains …

Well the love that Dad references must not have overridden our hurts. From the oldest to the youngest sibling, we speak to Dad out of respect. The Bible says to honor your father and your mother. It is the commandment with promise. We want to live long in the land. We love him and pray for him, and I believe the feeling is mutual. We love him, but we continue to pray for his and our deliverance. Lord deliver us from the hand of the enemy.

CHAPTER 14

The light switch came on. Mom had purchased a car for new husband. One day he decided to let some guys who had given him some drugs drive the car for the day. The day rental was Tom's method of payment for drugs.

When the drug dealers drove it, they wrecked it. The car was totaled; Tom could not explain this mishap away. After six months of marriage, Mom filed for an annulment. Tom didn't put up a fight. He knew Mom had had it with the relationship.

Tom was gone. We got our mom back. Dad was relieved. The family was comforted and mom was liberated again.

Dad's heart surgery was a success. The doctors had successfully carved his chest from his neck to below his stomach, repaired the damage, and sewed him shut.

The physical therapy would help him to strengthen his organs and muscles. The sabbatical away from the church would help him to clear his mind in preparation for the next challenge. But who and what would repair the damage done to the Carnegie clan?

Mom continues to work at the factory, and preach the gospel. But at times she still relates her dismay and hurt at the demonic destruction of the Carnegie family clan.

All of Dad's siblings but one have passed away. Their deaths are the result of alcohol abuse and smoking cigarettes. The one who remains is battling lung and liver cancer. Dad is so unhappy with his home life that he drinks the day and night away. My siblings have informed me that vodka is his drink of choice.

Although he has had a successful heart surgery, there are some guidelines that he is supposed to follow, such as no drinking or smoking. He does both. He is supposed to eat healthy, nutritious meals and exercise. Aubrey has conveniently taken red meat out of his diet. He just eats fish and sometimes chicken. Aubrey sits by, joins in, and watches him slowly drown himself in misery, guilt, shame, and dissipation.

None of us kids like to visit with them. The encounter is a solemn reminder of the selfishness and sorrow inflicted on us and Mom. According to Dad, the church is growing in record numbers. Yet when I visit, I witness the same ole faces. He preaches the Word, yet with the pollution of liquor, lust, and lack. The zeal and love that he once had has since waned.

I am divorced, the mother of twin boys, and a college professor. Caren is separated, a mother of two, and a high school teacher. Tonya is a single, still-looking-for-love mother of three, and an executive assistant to a public transportation company. Preston II is a twice-divorced father of two. He is a factory worker and up and coming nationally and internationally known Christian rapper. Felicia is going for her graduate degree and living in Florida. Grover is a married father of three and works for a travel agency. He has been called into the ministry to preach.

Grover is also an up and coming playwright. Katie is a single mother of twin girls and works for a youth activities center. Shawnee is a single mother of three and works as a life training skills educator.

Some of the siblings smoke cigarettes, some marijuana, some drink alcohol, some fornicate, yet we still believe in the power of the Holy Spirit. Some are realizing and experiencing complete deliverance from generational curses and demonic influences. Most importantly, it is the symmetry of God, faith, and prayer that will bring us all to an expectant end. I believe it. This is the reason I have written this book.

The Holy Bible says to train up a child in the way he should go and when he is old, he will not depart from it. We believe and we will continue to pray the devil to be rebuked and cast out of the Carnegie family, as we did for my Dad and Mom. We are calling those things that are not as though they were. We will win. The battle is not ours, but it is the Lord's.

Proverbs 11:29 reads, "He who brings trouble on his family will inherit only wind, and the fool will be servant to the wise." While it looks like the family is blowing in the wind, *Royalty Reigns : In the Grand Scheme of Things*, and God is still faithful.

About the Author

I reside in southern Ohio with my blessed and courageous twin boys. Since retiring from teaching for twelve years in higher education, I started Kingdom Pursuits, Inc., a consulting, grant writing, motivational speaking, and best-selling author business.

I look forward to the platform that God has given me to continue to proclaim the good news to every creature.